THE DARK
AT THE TOP
OF THE STAIRS

BY WILLIAM INGE

★ ACTING EDITION

★

**DRAMATISTS
PLAY SERVICE
INC.**

For Tennessee Williams

THE CAST

CORA FLOOD, a young housewife
RUBIN FLOOD, her husband
SONNY FLOOD, the ten-year-old son
REENIE FLOOD, the sixteen-year old daughter
FLIRT CONROY, a flapper friend of Reenie's
MORRIS LACEY, Cora's brother-in-law
LOTTIE LACEY, Cora's older sister
PUNKY GIVENS, Flirt's boy friend
SAMMY GOLDENBAUM, Punky's friend
CHAUFFEUR
BOY OUTSIDE

THE DARK AT THE TOP OF THE STAIRS was first presented by Saint Subber and Elia Kazan at the Music Box Theater, New York City, on December 5, 1957. It was directed by Mr. Kazan, the setting was by Ben Edwards and the lighting by Jean Rosenthal. The cast was as follows:

RUBIN FLOOD ....*Pat Hingle*
CORA FLOOD ....*Teresa Wright*
SONNY FLOOD ....*Charles Saari*
BOY OFFSTAGE ....*Jonathan Shawn*
REENIE FLOOD ....*Judith Robinson*
FLIRT CONROY ....*Evans Evans*
MORRIS LACEY ....*Frank Overton*
LOTTIE LACEY ....*Eileen Heckart*
SAMMY GOLDENBAUM ....*Timmy Everett*
PUNKY GIVENS ....*Carl Reindel*
CHAUFFEUR ....*Anthony Ray*

ACT I

The setting for the entire play is the home of Rubin Flood and his wife and two children, in a small Oklahoma town close to Oklahoma City. The time is the early nineteen-twenties, during an oil boom in the area. The house is comfortable and commodious, with probably eight or nine rooms. It is one of those square, frame houses built earlier in the century that stand secure as blocks, symbols of respectability and material comfort.

All we see of the Floods' house is the living room, where the action of the play takes place. There is a flight of stairs at the far left. At the top of them is the upstairs hallway which is not accessible to windows and sunlight. During the day time scenes, this small area is in semi-darkness and at night is black. We are conscious of this area throughout the play, as though it held some possible threat to the characters.

On the far Right, downstairs, is the outside entrance with a small hallway one must go through before coming into the living room.

In the middle of the living room is a wicker table, and two comfortable wicker chairs placed one on each side. Up stage center are sliding doors leading into the parlor, where we see a player piano. To the left of these doors and under the stairway, is a swinging door leading into the dining room. Extreme down stage left is a fireplace and a large comfortable leather chair. This area is considered Rubin's. In the rest of the room are book-shelves, a desk, a few small tables and portraits of Cora Flood's mother and father. There is a feeling of order and comfort in the room. When the curtain goes up, it is a late Monday afternoon in the early spring, about five o'clock. Outside, the sun is setting but the room is still filled with soft, warm light.

The curtain rises on a bare stage. Cora and Rubin are both upstairs, he is preparing to leave on a business trip.

CORA. (*Off L.*) Rubin!

RUBIN. (*Off L.*) Yah!

CORA. (*Off L.*) How many times do I have to tell you to rinse your hands before you dry them on a towel? You leave the bathroom looking like a wild horse had been using it. (*Rubin laughs*) I can smell the bay rum clear over here. My! You're certainly getting spruced up!

RUBIN. (*Starting down stairs carrying a suitcase. He is quite a good looking man of 36, still robust, dressed in western clothes*) I got to look good for my customers.

CORA. (*Calling down*) How long will you be gone this time?

RUBIN. I oughta be home end of the week. Saturday.

CORA. (*Calling down*) That's better than you usually do. Where will you be?

RUBIN. (*In his corner D.L., where he keeps his business paraphernalia*) I've made out my route for ya. I've left it on the mantle.

NEWSBOY. (*Off R.*) Hey, Mr. Flood. Jonsey says your tire's ready at the garage.

RUBIN. O.K. Ed, I'll be down to get it.

CORA. (*Coming down stairs*) Rubin, you've waited this long to go, why don't you wait now until morning? Here it is almost supper time. You won't be able to see any customers tonight, no matter where you go. Wait until morning. I'll get up early and fix you breakfast. I'll fix you biscuits, Rubin.

RUBIN. I shoulda been out first thing this morning. Monday, and I'm just gettin' away. I can make it to Muskogee tonight and be there first thing in the morning. I can finish up by noon and then get on to Chicasha.

CORA. I wish you were home more, Rubin.

RUBIN. I gotta make a livin'.

CORA. Other men make a living without travelling all over the country selling harness.

RUBIN. The way other men make a livin' is *their* business. I gotta make mine the best way I know how. I can't be no school master like your old man was when he brung you all out here from Pennsylvania. I can't be no dentist like your brother-in-law Morris. I was raised on a ranch and thought I'd spend my life on it. Sellin' harness is about all I'm prepared for . . . as long as there's any harness to sell.

CORA. (*With a trace of self-pity*) I envy women who have their husbands with them all the time. I never have anyone to take me any place. I live like a widow.

RUBIN. What do you want me to do? Give up my job and stay home here to pleasure you every day.

CORA. (*She is often disturbed by his language*) Rubin! Don't say that.

RUBIN. Jesus Christ, ya talk like a man had nothin' else to do but stay home and entertain you.

CORA. Rubin! It's not just myself I'm thinking of. It's the children. We have a daughter sixteen years old now. Do you realize that? Yes. Reenie's sixteen. And Sonny's ten. Sometimes they act like they didn't have a father.

RUBIN. (*Sits at table C. to sharpen his knife*) You're always tellin' me how good they do at school. The girl plays the piano, don't she? And the boy does something, too. Gets up and speaks pieces, or somethin' like that? (*Finds a sock in Cora's sewing basket on which to wipe his knife*)

CORA. (*Again she is shocked*) Rubin! Not on a clean sock!

RUBIN. Seems to me you all get along all right without me.

CORA. (*Sits in other chair C.*) Rubin, I worry about them. Reenie's so shy of people her own age, I don't know what to make of her. She's got no confidence at all. And I don't know how to give her any, but you could. Her eyes light up like candles every time you go near her.

RUBIN. (*A little embarrassed*) Come on now, Cora.

CORA. It's true . . . and the boy. Other boys tease him and call him names, Rubin. He doesn't know how to get along with them.

RUBIN. He oughta beat the tar outta the other boys.

CORA. He's not like you, Rubin. He's not like anyone I ever knew. He needs a father, Rubin. So does Reenie. Kids need a father when they're growing up, same as they need a mother.

RUBIN. You din allus talk like that. God almighty, when those kids was born, you hugged 'em so close to ya, ya made me think they was your own personal property, and I din have nothin' to do with 'em at all.

9

CORA. Rubin, that's not so.

RUBIN. The hell it ain't. Ya pampered 'em so much and coddled 'em, they thought I was just bein' mean if I tried to drill some sense into their heads.

CORA. Rubin. Don't say that.

RUBIN. You're always kissing and makin' over the boy until I sometimes wonder who's top man around here.

CORA. Rubin!

RUBIN. (*Rising*) I just said, I wonder.

CORA. If I kept the kids too close to me, it's only because you weren't there, and I had to have *someone* close to me. I had to have *some*one.

RUBIN. You're like an old mare Pa used to have on the ranch. Never wanted to give up her colts. By God, she'd keep 'em locked inside her and make all us men dig inside her with our hands to get 'em out. She never wanted to let 'em go.

CORA. (*A little repelled by the comparison*) Rubin, I don't like what you just said.

RUBIN. Well, she was a good mare in every other way.

CORA. You talk shamefully at times.

RUBIN. Well . . . I got my own way of sayin' things and it's pretty hard to change.

CORA. (*Watching him primp before the mirror*) You like being out on the road, don't you? You like to pretend you're still a young cowboy.

RUBIN. It wasn't a bad life.

CORA. Rubin, there are ever so many things you could do in town. Mr. Binny down here on the corner, makes a very good living just selling groceries to the neighborhood people. We could find a store like that, Rubin, and the kids and I could help you, too. You'd be happier doing something like that, Rubin. I know you would.

RUBIN. Don't tell me how t'be happy. I told you over and over, I ain't gonna spend my life cooped up in no store.

CORA. Or a filling station, Rubin. You could run a filling station or a garage. . . .

RUBIN. God damn it, Cora. I don't mean to have that kinda life. I just wasn't cut out for it. Now quit pickin' at me. We been mar-

10

ried seventeen years now. It seems t'me, you'd be ready t'accept me the way I am, or start lookin' for a new man.

CORA. (*Moving to him*) I don't want a new man. You know that.

RUBIN. Then start tryin' to put up with the one you got.

CORA. I do try.

RUBIN. Cause he ain't gonna change. Kiss me g'by. (*Playfully rough with her*) You come here and kiss me. (*He grabs her in a fast embrace and they kiss*)

CORA. (*Cautiously*) Rubin, you've got to leave me some money.

RUBIN. How much you gonna need?

CORA. Uh—could you let me have maybe, twenty-five dollars?

RUBIN. (*Hitting the ceiling*) Twenty-five dollars? I'm only gonna be gone till Saturday.

CORA. I have a lot of expenses this week, and—

RUBIN. *I* pay the bills.

CORA. I take care of the utilities, Rubin. And we have a big gas bill this month, last month was so cold. And Reenie's invited to a big birthday party out at the country club. The Ralston girl, and Reenie has to take her a present.

RUBIN. Me? Buy presents for Harry Ralston's girl when he owns half this town?

CORA. I don't often ask for this much.

RUBIN. (*Taking a bill from his wallet*) Twenty's the best I can do.

CORA. Thank you, Rubin. The Ralstons are giving Mary Jane a big dance. (*Finding a button loose on his coat*) Here let me fix that.

RUBIN. Cora, that'll be all right.

CORA. It'll only take a minute, sit down. (*They sit C. and Cora takes needle and thread from her sewing basket*) They're having a dance orchestra from Oklahoma City.

RUBIN. Harry and Peg Ralston puttin' on the dog now, are they?

CORA. Oh yes. I hardly ever see Peg any more.

RUBIN. I guess they don't have time for any of their old friends now that they've got so much money.

CORA. Anyway, they've asked Reenie to the party, I'm thankful for that.

11

RUBIN. The country club, huh? By God, I'd die in the poor house 'fore I'd ever do what Harry Ralston done.

CORA. Now, Rubin . . .

RUBIN. I mean it. He shot hisself in the foot to collect enough insurance money to make his first investment in oil.

CORA. Do you believe all those stories?

RUBIN. Hell, yes, I believe it. I know it for a fact. He shot hisself in the foot. He oughta be in jail now. Instead he's a social leader, givin' parties out at the country club. And I'm supposed to feel real proud he invited my daughter. Hurry up.

CORA. I ran into Peg down town during the winter. My, she was wearing a beautiful fur coat. Gray squirrel. And she was wearing a lot of lovely jewelry too.

RUBIN. She's spendin' his money as fast as Old Harry makes it.

CORA. Why shouldn't she have a few nice things?

RUBIN. They tell me they both started drinkin' now. They go out to those country club parties and get drunk as lords.

CORA. Peg didn't used to be like that.

RUBIN. They're all like that now. The town's gone oil-boom crazy. Chamber of Commerce says we're the wealthiest town per-capita in all the Southwest. I guess they're not exaggerating much, either, with all this oil money, those damned Indians riding around in their limosines gettin' all that money from the government, millions of dollars. Millions of dollars and nobody knows what to do with it. Come on, hurry up now . . .

CORA. (*Finishing with the button*) Rubin, if you want to make an investment, if you should hear of something absolutely sure, you can take that money Mama left me when she died. Two thousand dollars, Rubin. You can make an investment with that.

RUBIN. There ain't no such thing as a *sure thing* in the oil business.

CORA. Isn't there?

RUBIN. No. Ya can make a million dollars or lose your ass overnight.

CORA. Rubin, you don't have to use words like that.

RUBIN. I do a good job a supportin' ya, don't I?

CORA. Of course.

RUBIN. Then let's let well enough alone.

CORA. I was only thinking, it makes you feel kind of left out to be poor these days. (*Suddenly from outside R., we hear the sounds of young boys' jeering voices*)
BOYS' VOICES.
> Sonny Flood! His name is mud!
> Sonny runs home to Mama!
> Sonny plays with paper dolls!
> Sonny Flood, his name is mud!

CORA. See there! (*She jumps up nervously and runs outside R. to face her son's accostors*) You boys run along. My Sonny hasn't done anything to hurt you. You go home now or I'll call your mothers, every last one of you. You should be ashamed of yourselves, picking on a boy who's smaller than you are. (*Sonny comes running into the house now. (R.) It is hard to discern his feelings*)
RUBIN. (*Follows Cora out to the porch R.*) Cora, cut it out.
CORA. I can't stand quietly by while they're picking on my boy!
RUBIN. It's his battle. He's gotta fight it out for himself.
CORA. If they touch one hair of that boy's head I'll destroy them.
VOICE. (*One last heckler*) Sonny Flood, his name is mud!
CORA. I'll destroy them. (*Cora re-enters house*)
VOICE. Sonny Flood, his name is mud.
RUBIN. (*Still on the porch*) Hey, come here you fat butterball.
BOY. Hi, Mr. Flood.
RUBIN. How you doin', Jonathan? Let me see how you're growin'. (*He lifts the boy up*) Gettin' fat as a pig. Say hello to your Pa for me. (*The boy runs off and Rubin returns inside*)
CORA. Sonny, did they hurt you?
SONNY. No.
CORA. What started it this time?
SONNY. I don't know.
CORA. Did you say anything to make them mad?
SONNY. No.
CORA. They're just jealous because you make better grades than they do. They're just jealous, the little beasts.
RUBIN. Son!
SONNY. Huh?
RUBIN. Want me to teach you how to put up a good fight?
SONNY. (*Turning away from his father*) I don't think so.

13

RUBIN. (*To Cora*) What else can I do? Buy him a shotgun?

CORA. There should be *something* we can do. *Something*.

RUBIN. Everybody's gotta figure out his own way of handling things, Cora. Whether he fights or whether he runs.

CORA. I hate for anything to make me feel so helpless.

RUBIN. I gotta be goin'.

CORA. Say goodbye to your father, Sonny.

RUBIN. Goodbye, Son.

SONNY. (*Diffidently*) G'by.

RUBIN. (*Giving up*) Oh, hell.

CORA. Isn't there anything you can say to him?

RUBIN. Cora, if that boy wants me to help him, he's gotta come to me and tell me how. I never know what's on his mind.

CORA. You're just not interested.

RUBIN. Oh, hell, I give up. I plain give up. (*Exasperated, Rubin bolts outside R. Cora following him anxiously to the door*)

CORA. Rubin . . . Rubin . . . (*We hear Rubin's car drive off R. Cora returns C.*) Why don't you listen to your father, Sonny? Why don't you let him help you?

SONNY. Where's Reenie?

CORA. (*Sitting*) She's downtown. Your father isn't here very often, why don't you try and get along with him when he is?

SONNY. (*Wanting to evade the issue*) I don't know.

CORA. Most boys your age *worship* their fathers.

SONNY. I like him all right. Where are my movie stars?

CORA. Forget your movie stars for a minute. You have a father to be proud of, Sonny. He and his family were pioneers. They fought Indians and buffalo, and they settled this country when it was just a wilderness. Why, if there was a movie about them, you couldn't wait to see it.

SONNY. Mom, it just makes it worse when you come out and tell those boys you're going to call their mothers.

CORA. You just won't listen to me, will you? You just won't listen to anyone. You're so set in your ways.

SONNY. I want my movie stars.

CORA. I put them in the bookshelves when I was straightening up this morning. The only pasttime you have is coming home here and playing with those pictures of movie stars. (*Sonny gets out his scrapbook and spreads it on the floor*)

SONNY. I like them.

CORA. That's all the friends you have. Not real friends at all. Just *pictures* of all the lovely friends you'd *like* to have. There's a mighty big difference between pictures of people and the way people really are.

SONNY. I like pictures.

CORA. Maybe you should get out and play with the other boys more often, Sonny.

SONNY. They play stupid games.

CORA. People distrust you if you don't play the same games they do, Sonny. It's the same after you grow up.

SONNY. I'm not going to play games just to make them like me.

CORA. (*Suddenly warm and affectionate*) Come to me, Sonny. I wish I understood you better, boy.

SONNY. I don't see why.

CORA. (*Caressing him*) No, I don't suppose you do. You're a speckled egg, and the old hen that laid you can't help wondering how you got in the nest. But I love you, Sonny. More than anything else in the world.

SONNY. Mom, can I go to a movie tonight?

CORA. You know the rules. One movie a week, on Friday night.

SONNY. Please, Mom. It's a real special movie tonight. Honest, I just *got* to see it.

CORA. Oh, I bet. It's always something special and you've just got to see it like your very life depended on it. No. You're supposed to study on week nights. Now, stay home and study.

SONNY. I've already got all my lessons.

CORA. You have to speak at Mrs. Stamford's tea party next Saturday. Why don't you memorize a new recitation?

SONNY. I can't find anything I like.

CORA. Oh! I found a cute little poem in the Oklahoma City paper this morning. It's about a little boy who hates to take castor oil. It starts off:

"Of all the nasty things, gee whiz!
I think the very worst there is . . ."

SONNY. (*Obviously bored*) I want to do something serious.

15

CORA. Serious! Like what?

SONNY. I dunno.

CORA. Goodness, it seems to me we've got enough serious things in the world without you getting up to recite sad pieces. (*Outside the window (L.), we see Flirt and Reenie come onto the porch, giggling*)

SONNY. I'm tired of all those stupid pieces you cut out of the papers.

CORA. My goodness! Aren't we getting superior! Oh, here's your sister, Sonny. Be a little gentleman and open the door for her.

REENIE. (*Sticking her head in through the door, asking cautiously*) Is Daddy gone, Mom?

CORA. Yes, he's gone. The coast is clear.

REENIE. (*Runs to Cora excitedly. She is a plain girl with no conscious desire of being anything else*) Oh, Mom, it's the prettiest dress I ever had.

CORA. (*Rising*) Bring it in.

REENIE. Come on in, Flirt.

FLIRT. (*Enters carrying a large dress box. She is a young flapper of the era*) Hello, Mrs. Flood.

CORA. Hello, Flirt. (*Flirt opens the box*)

REENIE. And they took up the hem and took in the waist so that it fits me just perfectly now.

FLIRT. I think it's simply scrumptious, Mrs. Flood.

CORA. Thank you, Flirt. Hold it up, Reenie.

FLIRT. Yes, hold it up.

REENIE. (*Holding the dress before her*) Is Dad going to be awfully mad, Mom?

CORA. I told you, he's not going to know anything about it for a while, Reenie. He gave me some money before he left, enough for me to make a small down payment. My, I bet Flirt thinks we're terrible plotting this way.

FLIRT. Shucks, no. Mama and I do the same thing.

REENIE. Oh, Mom. You should see the dress Flirt got.

FLIRT. It's all red, with spangles on it, and a real short skirt. It's just darling. Daddy says he feels like disowning me in it.

CORA. Did you buy your dress at Delman's too, Flirt.

16

FLIRT. (*She can't help boasting an advantage*) No. Mama takes me into Oklahoma City to buy all my clothes.

CORA. Oh!

SONNY. (*Feeling the dress*) Look, it's got stars.

REENIE. (*Snapping angrily*) Sonny, take your dirty hands off my new dress.

SONNY. (*Ready to start a fight anytime Reenie is*) My hands are *not* dirty! So there.

REENIE. You make me mad. Why don't you go outdoors and play ball instead of staying in the house all the time, watching everything I do. Mother, why don't you make him go out and play?

SONNY. It's my house as much as it's yours, and I've got as much right to be here as you do. I don't like you. I hate you, so there.

CORA. (*Always distressed by their fighting*) Reenie. He only wanted to touch the dress. He likes pretty things too.

FLIRT. Gee whiz, he hasn't done anything, Reenie.

CORA. Of course he hasn't. You kids are just antagonistic to each other. You scrap all the time.

SONNY. I hate you.

REENIE. I hate you too.

CORA. Now stop that. Is that any way for a brother and sister to talk? I'm not going to have any more of it. Flirt? Are you taking the Ralston girl a birthday present?

FLIRT. Mama got me a compact to give her. It's the only thing we could think of. She already has everything under the sun.

CORA. Yes, I suppose so. Her parents are so wealthy now. Well, I'll have to shop for something for Reenie to take her.

FLIRT. You know, my folks knew the Ralstons before he made all his money. Mama says Mrs. Ralston used to clerk in a millinery store downtown.

CORA. Yes, I knew her then.

FLIRT. And my daddy says that Mr. Ralston was so crazy to make money in oil that he shot himself in the foot. Isn't that awful?

SONNY. Why did he do that? (*Reenie goes into the parlor U.C. to try on dress. Sonny sits C. table. Flirt fascinates him. He could listen to her forever*)

FLIRT. So he could collect enough insurance money to make his first investment in oil. Did you hear that story, too, Mrs. Flood?

17

CORA. Oh yes . . . you hear all kinds of stories about the Ralstons now.

FLIRT. And you know, some of the women out at the country club didn't want to give Mr. Ralston a membership because they disapproved of *her*.

CORA. Is that so?

FLIRT. But when you've got as much money as the Ralstons do, I guess you can be a member of *anything*. I just hate Mary Jane Ralston. Some of the boys at school think she's pretty but I think she's a *cow*. I'm not being jealous, either. I guess if I had as much money to spend on clothes as she does, I'd have been voted the prettiest girl in school, too. Anyway, I'm absolutely positive she peroxides her hair.

CORA. Really?

REENIE. (*Poking her head out between the sliding doors U.C.*) Are you sure?

FLIRT. Yes. Because she and I play on the same volley ball team in gym class, and her locker is right next to mine, and . . .

CORA. (*Reminding her of Sonny's presence*) Flirt!

FLIRT. Isn't it terrible for me to say all these things, when I'm going to her birthday party? But I don't care. She just invited me because she had to. Because my daddy's her daddy's lawyer.

SONNY. (*As Reenie comes out of parlor U.C. wearing her new dress, he makes a grotesque face and props his feet on the table*) Uggh . . .

CORA. Oh, Reenie! it's lovely—Sonny, take your feet down. Let me see! Oh, Reenie. He did a fine job. Flirt! tell me more about the young man who's taking Reenie to the party.

FLIRT. He's a Jew, Mrs. Flood.

CORA. Oh, he is?

REENIE. Do you think it's all right for me to go out with a Jew, Mom?

CORA. Why of course, dear, if he's a nice boy.

FLIRT. His name is Sammy Goldenbaum, and he comes from Hollywood, California, and his mother's a moving picture actress.

CORA. Really?

REENIE. Flirt just found that out, Mom. I didn't know it before.

SONNY. (*All ears*) A moving picture actress!

18

FLIRT. Yes, but she just plays itsy-bitsy parts in pictures. I saw her once. She played a real stuck-up society woman, and she was Gloria Swanson's rival. You see, they were in love with the same man, Thomas Meighan, and she told all these lies about Gloria Swanson to make people think Gloria Swanson wasn't nice, so she could marry Thomas Meighan herself. But Thomas Meighan found out all about it, finally, and . . .

REENIE. Mom, what's a Jewish person like?

CORA. Well, I never knew many Jewish people, Reenie, but . . .

FLIRT. I've heard that some of them can be awful fast with girls.

CORA. I'm sure they're just like any other people.

FLIRT. (*Dancing coquettishly about room*) They don't believe in Christianity.

CORA. Most of them don't.

REENIE. But do they act different?

CORA. (*Not really knowing*) Well . . .

FLIRT. My daddy says they always try to get the best of you in business.

CORA. There are lots of very nice Jewish people, Reenie.

FLIRT. Oh sure! Gee whiz, of course.

REENIE. I don't know what to expect.

FLIRT. Kid, he's a *boy*. That's all you have to know.

CORA. There are Jewish families over in Oklahoma City, but I guess there aren't any here in town.

FLIRT. Oh yes there are, Mrs. Flood. The Lewises are Jewish, only they changed their name from Levin so no one would know.

CORA. I guess I did hear that some place.

REENIE. Mom, I feel sort of scared to go out with someone so different.

FLIRT. Oh, you're crazy, Reenie. Gee whiz, I'd never go steady with a Jewish boy, but I'd sure take a date with one—if I didn't have any other way of going.

CORA. Now Reenie, I'm sure that any friend of the Givens boy is nice, whether he's Jewish or not. And besides, his mother's a movie actress. Think of that.

FLIRT. Yes, but not a famous one.

CORA. (*To Reenie*) Now, you have a nice date to the party, and

19

a lovely new dress to wear. You can be sure you'll have a good time.

FLIRT. Gosh, yes! After all, a party's a party. And it's out at the Country Club, and they're having a swell dance orchestra from Oklahoma City, and they're giving favors. I can't wait. Fix your hair real cute and you'll look all right. (*Looks at her wrist watch*) Oh, heck! I've got to go home.

CORA. Do you want to stay here for supper, Flirt?

FLIRT. No. It's my night to fix supper for the folks. My mother makes me fix supper once a week, cook's night out. She says it's good for me to learn something about homemaking. Isn't that crazy? The only thing I know how to cook is salmon loaf. I learned how to make it in Domestic Science class. I've made salmon loaf every Monday night now for the whole year. Kid, can you help me study for that stupid old civics test we're having next week?

REENIE. I guess so.

FLIRT. Civics! Why can't they teach us something in that old school that'd do us some good?

CORA. Goodbye, Flirt.

FLIRT. Goodbye, Mrs. Flood, goodbye, Reenie. Oh, Sonny, you come over to *my* house and play sometime. I know how to be nice to little boys.

CORA. Goodbye. (*Flirt exits R.*) Sonny, you've got to go to the store now if we're going to have anything for supper tonight.

SONNY. Mom! Can I get a candy bar?

CORA. Wouldn't you rather have the nickel to put in your piggy bank?

SONNY. No— I want a candy bar.

CORA. All right. If you promise not to eat it before supper.

REENIE. I want one too. I want a nut-hershey.

CORA. Bring one for Reenie, too.

SONNY. She can get her own candy bar.

REENIE. He's mean, Mom.

SONNY. I don't care. She makes me mad, and I don't like her.

CORA. Sonny, she's your sister.

SONNY. I don't care. I don't like her. (*Exits R.*)

CORA. Oh, God, some day you kids are going to be sorry. When you can't even get along with people in your own family, how can you expect to get along with people out in the world? (*Looks out the window protectively*) Poor Sonny, every time he leaves the house, those neighborhood bullies pick on him. I guess they've all gone home now. (*Reenie has taken off her new dress and throws it on a chair*)

REENIE. I don't know if I like Flirt or not.

CORA. (*Comes away from window*) Why, what's the matter?

REENIE. The only reason she likes me is because I help her with her studies. (*Reenie goes into parlor U.C., gets her daytime clothes and comes back to put them on*)

CORA. Why do you say that?

REENIE. I just do.

CORA. You don't think *anyone* likes you, do you?

REENIE. Mom, maybe we shouldn't have bought the dress.

CORA. What?

REENIE. I mean it, Mom. Dad'd be awful mad if he knew.

CORA. I told you, he's not going to know.

REENIE. Won't he be here the night of the party?

CORA. No. And even if he were, he wouldn't notice the dress was new unless you told him about it.

REENIE. Just the same, Mom, I don't feel right about it.

CORA. Why don't you feel right?

REENIE. Because . . . the dress cost so much, and what good is it going to do me? I never have a good time at those dances, anyway. No one ever dances with me.

CORA. This time it's going to be different. You've got a new dress, and you've got a nice young man coming here all the way from California to be your escort. Think of it. Why, most young girls would be too excited to breathe.

REENIE. It's just a *blind* date.

CORA. What are you talking about?

REENIE. They give blind dates to all the girls in town that nobody else wants to take.

CORA. Daughter, I'm sure that's not so.

REENIE. Oh, Mom, you just don't know.

CORA. I do, too.

REENIE. Besides, he's Jewish. I never knew a Jewish boy before. I'm scared.

21

CORA. Daughter, you're just looking for excuses. You just don't want to go, do you? Reenie, don't you want to have friends?

REENIE. Yes, but . . .

CORA. You're not going to make friends just staying home playing the piano, or going to the library studying your lessons. I'm glad you're studious and talented, but those things aren't enough just in themselves.

REENIE. I don't want to talk about it any more.

CORA. You're going to have to talk about these things some day. Where are you going?

REENIE. To practice the piano. (*Goes into the parlor U.C. and starts playing scales*)

CORA. (*Angrily impatient*) That's where you spend half your life, *practicing* at the piano. (*Reenie bangs on piano and exits to dining room U.L.*) But will you get up and play for people so they'll know how talented you are? No. You hide your light under a bushel. You stay home and play behind closed doors, where no one can hear you except your own family. All you do is *pity* yourself at the piano. That's all. You go in there and pity yourself, playing all those sad pieces. (*Reenie comes out of dining room—Crosses to fireplace and waters her plants*)

REENIE. Mom, I just couldn't get up before an audience and play. I just couldn't.

CORA. Why couldn't you? What good is it for your father to have bought the piano? What use is it? (*Reenie begins to sob*) Now, don't cry, Reenie. I'm sorry. (*Reenie goes into parlor U.C. and resumes her monotonous scales. Cora goes to telephine D.L.*) Long distance? Give me 3607-J in Oklahoma City, please. (*There is a wait of several moments*) Hello, Lottie. . . . Lottie, can you and Morris come over to dinner Friday night? I haven't seen you for so long, I want to talk with you, Lottie. I've just got to see some of my own flesh and blood. (*We hear Rubin's car slam to a stop outside R., the car door slams and then he comes stamping up to the front porch R.*) Reenie's going to a big party out at the country club, and I thought I'd have a nice dinner first. . . . Rubin won't be here and I'll want company. Please come. Oh, I'm so glad. I'll be looking forward to seeing you.

RUBIN. (*Bursting into the house*) What the hell's been goin' on

22

behind my back? (*Sees the innocent dress lying on a chair*) There it is!

CORA. (*Her phone call ended*) Rubin!

RUBIN. (*Displaying the dress as evidence*) So this is what ya wanted the extra money for. Fine feathers! Fine feathers! And ya buy 'em when my back is turned.

CORA. Rubin, we were going to tell you. . . .

RUBIN. A man has to go downtown and talk with some of his pals before he knows what's goin' on in his own family.

CORA. Who told you?

RUBIN. That's all right who told me. I got my own ways a findin' out what goes on when my back is turned.

CORA. You didn't leave town at all. You've been down to that dirty old pool hall.

RUBIN. I got a right to go to the pool hall whenever I damn please.

CORA. I thought you were in such a hurry to get out of town. Oh, yes, you had to get to Muskogee tonight.

RUBIN. I can still make it to Muskogee. (*Finds the price tag on the dress*) $19.75! Lord have mercy! $19.75.

CORA. (*Approaching Rubin*) Did Loren Delman come into the pool hall while you were there? Did he? Did he tell you? If he did I'll never buy anything in that store again.

RUBIN. That'd suit me just fine.

CORA. Oh, why couldn't he have kept his mouth shut? I was going to pay for the dress a little at a time, and . . .

RUBIN. "The finest dress I had in the store," he says, walking into the arcade with a big cigar stuck in his mouth, wearin' a suit of fine tailored clothes. "I just sold your wife the finest dress I had in the store."

CORA. Oh, that makes me furious.

RUBIN. Jesus Christ woman, whatta you take me for, one a those millionaire oil men? Is that what you think you're married to?

REENIE. (*Pokes her head in through parlor door U.C., speaking with tears and anxiety*) I told you he'd be mad, Mom. Let's take the dress back, Mom. I don't want to go to the party anyhow.

CORA. (*Angrily impatient*) Get back in that parlor, Reenie, and don't come in here until I tell you do. (*Slams parlor doors shut*)

23

RUBIN. See there! That girl don't even want the dress. It's *you*, puttin' all these high-fallutin' ideas in her head about parties, and dresses and nonsense.

CORA. Rubin, of course Reenie doesn't want to go to the party. She never wants to go any place. All she wants to do is lock herself in the parlor and practice at the piano, or go to the library and hide her nose in a book. After all, she's going to want to get married one of these days, isn't she? And where's she going to look for a husband? In the public library? (*Rubin goes to his corner, D.L., sits in his big leather chair, and draws a pint of whiskey out of his desk drawer*)

RUBIN. I bought her a fine dress . . . just a little while back.

CORA. Oh, you did?

RUBIN. Yes, I did.

— CORA. That's news to me, when?

RUBIN. Just a few months ago. Sure I did.

CORA. I certainly never saw it. What'd it look like?

RUBIN. It was white.

CORA. Rubin Flood, that was the dress you bought her three years ago when she graduated from the eighth grade. And she hasn't had a new dress since then, except for a few school clothes.

RUBIN. Why couldn't she wear the white dress to the party?

CORA. Because she's grown three inches since you got her that dress, and besides I cut it up two years ago and dyed it black and made her a skirt out of it to wear with a middy.

RUBIN. Just the same, I ain't got money to throw away on no party togs. I just ain't got it.

CORA. Oh no. You don't have money when we need something here at home, do you?

RUBIN. I'm tellin' ya, right now I don't.

CORA. But you always have money for a bottle of bootleg whiskey when you want it, don't you? And I daresay, you've got money for a few other things, too, that I needn't mention just at present.

RUBIN. What're ya talkin' about?

CORA. *You* know what I'm talking about.

RUBIN. The hell I do.

CORA. I know what goes on when you go out on the road. You

24

may tell me you spruce up for your customers, but I happen to know better. Do you think I'm a fool?

RUBIN. I don't know what you're talkin' about.

CORA. I happen to have friends, decent, self-respecting people, who tell me a few things that happen when you visit Ponca City.

RUBIN. You mean the Werpel sisters!

CORA. It's all right, who I mean. I have friends over there. That's all I need to say.

RUBIN. Those nosey old maids, the Werpel sisters! God damn! Have they been runnin' to you with stories?

CORA. Maybe you don't have money to buy your daughter a new dress, but it seems you have money to take Mavis Pruitt to dinner whenever you're over there, and to a movie afterwards, and give her presents.

RUBIN. I've known Mavis . . . Pruitt ever since I was a boy! What harm is there if I take her to a movie?

CORA. You're always too tired to take *me* to a movie when you come home.

RUBIN. Life's different out on the road.

CORA. I bet it is.

RUBIN. Besides, I din ask her. She came into the Gibson House one night when I was havin' my dinner. What could I do but ask her to join me?

CORA. She went to the Gibson House because she knew *you* were there. I know what kind of woman she is.

RUBIN. She's not as bad as she's painted. That poor woman's had a hard time of it, too.

CORA. Oh, she has!

RUBIN. Yes she has. I feel sorry for her.

CORA. Oh, you do!

RUBIN. Yes, I do. Is there any law that says I can't feel sorry for Mavis Pruitt?

CORA. She's had her eye on you ever since I can remember.

RUBIN. Oh, 'shoot!

CORA. What happened to the man she left town with after we were married?

RUBIN. He run off and left her.

CORA. For good reason, too, I bet. I also heard that she was seen

25

sporting a pair of black-bottom hose shortly after you left town, and that you were seen buying such a pair of hose at the Globe Dry Goods Store.

RUBIN. By God, you got yourself a real detective service goin', haven't you?

CORA. I don't ask people to tell me these things. I wish to God they didn't.

RUBIN. All right, I bought her a pair of hose. I admit it. It was her birthday. The hose cost me sixty-eight cents. They made that poor woman happy. After all, I've known her ever since I was a boy. Besides, I was a li'l more flush then.

CORA. How do you think it makes me feel when people tell me things like that?

RUBIN. Ya oughtn'ta listen.

CORA. How can I help it?

RUBIN. (*He has to think to call her by her full name, to keep Cora from presuming too much familiarity between them*) There's nothing 'tween me and Mavis . . . Pruitt . . . Mavis Pruitt, nothin' for you to worry about.

CORA. There's probably a woman like her in every town you visit. That's why you want to get out of town, to go frisking over the country like a young stallion.

RUBIN. You just hush your mouth. The daughter'll hear you.

CORA. (*Indulging a little self-pity*) A lot you care about your daughter. A lot you care about any of us.

RUBIN. You don't think I care for ya unless I set ya on my knee and nuzzle ya.

CORA. What you need for a wife is a squaw. Why didn't you marry one of those Indian women out on the reservation? Yes. She'd make you rich now, too, wouldn't she? And you wouldn't have to pay any attention to her at all. (*Sonny is seen coming onto porch R.*)

RUBIN. All right. Maybe that's what I *shoulda* done.

CORA. Oh. So you want to throw it up to me!

RUBIN. Throw what? (*Sonny quietly enters room carrying a sack of groceries. Cora and Rubin are too far into battle to notice him*)

CORA. You know what, Rubin Flood.

RUBIN. I don't know nothin'.

CORA. You never *wanted* to marry me.

RUBIN. I never said that.

CORA. It's true, isn't it?

RUBIN. I'm tellin' ya, it ain't.

CORA. It is. I've felt it all these years. (*Sonny crosses and enters parlor U.C., still unobserved by Rubin and Cora*)

RUBIN. All right. If you're so determined to think it, then go ahead. I admit, in some ways I din wanna marry nobody. Can't ya understand how a man feels, givin' up his freedom?

CORA. And how does a woman feel, knowing her husband married her only because . . . because he . . . (*Cora now spots Reenie spying between the parlor doors U.C. She screams at her*) Reenie, get away from there!

RUBIN. None of this is what we was arguin' about in the first place. We was arguin' about the dress. Ya gotta take it back.

CORA. *I won't.*

RUBIN. *Ya will.*

CORA. Reenie's going to wear her new dress to the party, or you'll have to bury me.

RUBIN. You'll take that dress back to Loren Delman, or I'm leavin' this house for good and never comin' back.

CORA. Go on. You're only home half the time as it is. We can get along without you the rest of the time.

RUBIN. Then that's what you're gonna do. There'll be ice cream parlors in hell before I come back to this place and listen to your jaw. (*Bolts into the hallway now, far R.*)

CORA. Get out! Get out and go to Ponca City. Mavis Pruitt is waiting. She's probably getting lonesome without you. (*Sonny enters quietly from dining room U.L. and watches*)

RUBIN. By God, Cora, it's all I can do to keep from hittin' you when you talk like that.

CORA. (*Following him into hallway R., taunting him. Here they are both unseen by audience*) Go on and hit me! You wouldn't dare? (*But he does dare. We hear the sound of his blow which sends Cora reeling back into parlor*) Rubin! (*Reenie watches from parlor*)

RUBIN. I'll go to Ponca City, and drink booze and take Mavis to the movies, and raise every kind of hell I can think of. T'hell with you! (*He bolts outside*)

27

CORA. (*Running to the door*) Don't you ever set foot in this house again, Rubin Flood. I'll never forget what you've said. Never! Don't you ever come back inside this house again! (*We hear Rubin's car drive off now. Cora returns C. still too dazed to be sure what has happened*)

SONNY. Gee, Mom. That was the worst fight you ever had, wasn't it?

CORA. How long have you been standing there, Sonny?

SONNY. Since he hit you.

REENIE. (*Coming forth from parlor*) Did he mean it about not coming back? Oh, Mom, why did you have to say all those things? I love Daddy. Why do you say those things to him?

CORA. Oh God, I hate for you kids to see us fight this way.

SONNY. What did he mean, he didn't want to marry you?

CORA. You're not old enough to understand these things, Sonny.

SONNY. Did he hurt you, Mom. Did he?

CORA. I'm still too mad to know whether he did or not.

REENIE. I don't think he'll ever come back. What'll we do, Mom?

CORA. Now, don't worry Reenie.

REENIE. Will we have to go to the poor house?

CORA. No, of course not. Now quit worrying.

REENIE. But if Daddy doesn't come back?

CORA. I still have the money my mother left me, haven't I, and if worst comes to worst we can always go to Oklahoma City and move in with your Aunt Lottie and Uncle Morris.

SONNY. (*Jumping up and down in glee*) Goody, goody, goody. I wanta move to Oklahoma City.

REENIE. Listen to him, Mom. He's *glad* Daddy's gone. He's *glad*.

SONNY. I don't care. I wanna move to Oklahoma City.

REENIE. I don't. *This* is home. *This* is. And I don't want to move.

CORA. Now, children!

REENIE. I hate you.

SONNY. I hate you too. So there! Oklahoma City! Oklahoma City! I wanta move to Oklahoma City!

CORA. Stop it! There's been enough fighting in this house for one night. Reenie, take your dress upstairs and hang it in the closet.

REENIE. I hate the old dress now. It's the cause of all the trouble. I hate it.

CORA. You do what I tell you. You take that dress upstairs and hang it in the closet. You're going to go to that party if I have to take you there myself. (*Reenie starts upstairs L.*) The next time you're invited to a party, I'll let you go in a hand-me-down.

SONNY. (*With the joy of discovering a new continent*) Oklahoma City.

CORA. (*Wearily*) I'll go out and fix supper, although I don't imagine any of us will feel like eating.

SONNY. I do. I'm hungry.

CORA. (*A little amused*) Are you? Good. Come to me, Sonny! (*With a sudden need for affection*) Do you love me, Boy? Do you love your Old Mom?

SONNY. More than all the world with a fence around it.

CORA. (*Clasping him to her*) Oh God, what would I do without you kids? I hope you'll always love me, Sonny. I hope you always will. (*Reenie comes down stairs L.*) Where are you going, daughter? (*Sonny sits on floor, spreading out his picture collection*) (*Reenie looks disdainfully upon them, and marches into the parlor where, in a moment we hear her playing a lovely Chopin nocturne*)

SONNY. Mom, I'm going to sell my autographed photograph of Fatty Arbuckle. Millicent Dalrymple said she'd give me fifteen cents for it. And Fatty Arbuckle isn't one of my favorites any more. If I sold the photograph, I'd have enough to go to the movie tonight and buy a sack of popcorn, besides.

CORA. (*Lying on the floor beside him*) If the world was falling to pieces all about you, you'd still want to go to the movies, wouldn't you?

SONNY. I don't see why not.

CORA. Your mother's unhappy, Sonny. Doesn't that mean anything to you?

SONNY. Well . . . I'm sorry.

CORA. I want you kids near me tonight. Can't you understand? Oh, God, wouldn't it be nice if life were as sweet as music! (*For a moment, mother and son lie together in each other's arms. Then Cora stands, as though fearing her own indulgence, and takes Sonny by the hand*) Come! Help me set the table, Sonny.

CURTAIN

ACT II

At rise of curtain, we hear a banging rendition of "Smiles" coming from the parlor where Lottie is at the piano, Sonny by her side, both singing in hearty voices. Reenie stands listlessly watching, drying a dish. Morris sits far L. in Rubin's chair, working one of those baffling little hand puzzles that has got the best of him. Lottie proves to be a big, fleshy woman, a few years older than Cora. She wears a gaudy dress and lots of costume jewelry. Morris is a big defeated-looking man of wrecked virility.

LOTTIE AND SONNY. (*Singing*)
"There are smiles that make us happy
There are smiles that make us blue
There are smiles that steal away the teardrops
As the sunshine steals away the dew."

CORA. (*Coming from kitchen U.L.*) I won't need you to help me with the dishes, Reenie. I want you to go upstairs now and get ready for your party. (*Calls in parlor U.C.*) Sonny! Sonny!

MORRIS. Sure was a good dinner, Cora.

CORA. What, Morris?

MORRIS. (*Trying to make himself heard above the piano*) I said sure was a good dinner.

CORA. Thank you, Morris. Now go and get dressed, Reenie. (*She reluctantly goes upstairs L.*) Sonny! Sonny! Lottie, will you please stop that racket. A body can't hear himself think.

LOTTIE, SONNY. (*Finishing the chorus*)
But the smiles that fill my heart with sunshine
Are the smiles that you give to me.

CORA. Sonny, I said you've got to help me in the kitchen.

SONNY. Why can't Reenie?

CORA. She cleared the table for me, and now she has to bathe and get ready for her party.

30

SONNY. I have to do everything around here.

LOTTIE. (*In the voice one uses to indulge a child*) I think its a shame. (*Sonny and Cora exit into dining room U.L.*)'

LOTTIE. (*Coming from parlor*) Cora always was jealous because I could play the piano and she couldn't. (*Looks to see if Cora is out of hearing distance*) Do I have something to tell you! Do you know why she asked us over here? (*Hurries over to Morris D.L.*)

MORRIS. For dinner.

LOTTIE. No! She and Rubin have had another fight. She told me all about it while I was in the kitchen helping her get dinner on the table.

MORRIS. What about this time?

LOTTIE. About a new dress she bought for Reenie. But what difference does that make? They could fight about anything. Only this time he hit her.

MORRIS. He did?

LOTTIE. Don't tell her I tell you. Poor Cora. I guess maybe she has a hard time with Rubin.

MORRIS. Has Rubin walked out again?

LOTTIE. You guessed it. Do you know what she wants to do now, Honey? She wants to bring the kids over to Oklahoma City to live *with us?* She says I suggested they do that some time ago. I guess maybe I did, but my God, I never thought they'd do it. We'd be perfectly miserable with her and the two kids living with us, wouldn't we, Morris? With only one extra bedroom, one of 'em would have to sleep on the davenport in the living room, and then what would happen when your patients started coming in the morning.

MORRIS. Yah. It wouldn't work out very well.

LOTTIE. No. Oh my! The way she pampers those kids, Morris. If she had her way, she'd spoil 'em rotten.

MORRIS. What did you tell her, honey?

LOTTIE. Well, I haven't told her anything yet. I was so flabbergasted when she asked me. I just hemmed . . . (*Sonny enters the parlor U.C. to put away a big vase that Cora has just washed. Lottie sees him*) Hi! Honey.

SONNY. They got me working again.

LOTTIE. I think it's terrible. (*Sonny exits into dining room U.L.*)

. . . and hawed until I could think of something to say. Oh Morris, put away that puzzle and listen to me. She's going to come to you sometime this evening and ask you about it, and all you need to say is, "I'm leaving all that in Lottie's hands, Cora." Can you remember that? Just say it real nice, like it was none of your business.

MORRIS. I'll remember.

LOTTIE. You say you will, but will you?

MORRIS. Yes, honey.

LOTTIE. I don't know. You're so afraid of hurting people's feelings.

MORRIS. That's not so.

LOTTIE. Oh, it is too. Don't I know! You had to go to see some psychologist over in Oklahoma City because you were so afraid of hurting your patients when you drilled their teeth. Now confess it. It was actually making you sick, that you had to drill your patients' teeth and hurt them.

MORRIS. Honey, I wasn't really *sick* about it.

LOTTIE. You were too. Now remember what I say. Don't get *soft-hearted* at the last minute and tell Cora to bring the kids and come on over. My God, Morris, we'd be in the looney bin in less than two days with them in the house. Cora may be my own flesh and blood but I couldn't live with her to save my life. And I love those kids of her. I do, Morris. But I couldn't live with them. They'd drive me crazy. You, too. You know they would.

CORA. (*Enters the parlor U.C. to put napkins in the sideboard*) Almost finished.

LOTTIE. You shoulda let me help you. (*But Cora has returned to kitchen U.L.*) Cora said something to me about her getting a job at one of the big department stores over in Oklahoma City. Can you see her doin' a thing like that? I can't. "Cora," I said, "you wouldn't last two days at that kind of work, on your feet all day, taking people's sass." Well, I don't know if I convinced her or not, but I gave her something to think about. (*Sneaks back to parlor door to see if Cora is within earshot, then comes back to Morris speaking in a very confidential voice*) Morris? Do you think Rubin still plays around with Mavis Pruitt over in Ponca City?

MORRIS. (*Clamming up*) I don't know, honey.

LOTTIE. You do, too.

MORRIS. I'm telling you, I don't.

LOTTIE. You men, you tell each other everything, but you all want to protect each other. And wild horses and screaming ravens couldn't get you to talk.

MORRIS. Well, whatever Rubin does . . . like that . . . is *his* business.

LOTTIE. My! Don't we sound righteous all of a sudden! Well, I bet anything he still sees her.

MORRIS. Well, don't you let on to Cora.

LOTTIE. I won't. Did I ever tell you about the first time she met Rubin?

MORRIS. Yes, honey.

LOTTIE. I did not! Cora and I were coming out of the five-and-ten. She'd wanted to buy a little lace to put on a dress. And here comes Rubin, like a picture of Sin, riding down the street on a shiny black horse. My God, he was handsome. Neither of us knew who he was. But he looked at Cora and smiled, and Cora began to get all nervous and fluttery. And do you know what? He came by the house that very night and wanted to see her. Mama and Papa didn't know what to do. They stood around like they were afraid of Rubin. But Cora went out riding with him. He'd brought a buggy with him. And six weeks later they were married. Mama and Papa were worried sick. Rubin's people were all right, but they were ranchers. Kind of wild. And Cora only seventeen, not out of high school. I think that's the reason Papa had his stroke, don't you, Morris?

MORRIS. Maybe . . .

LOTTIE. I do. They just felt like Cora might as well be dead as married to a man like Rubin. But Cora was always a determined creature. Mama and Papa were no match for her when she wanted her own way.

MORRIS. Well, I like Rubin.

LOTTIE. I do too, honey. I'm not saying anything against him. And he's made a lot better husband than I ever thought he would. But I'm glad *I'm* not married to him. I'd be worried to death all the time. I'm glad I'm married to a nice man I can trust. (*Morris*

33

does not know how to respond to this endearment. He crosses the room troubledly)

MORRIS. What'll Cora do if Rubin doesn't come back?

LOTTIE. Well, that's not our problem, Honey.

MORRIS. Yes, but just the same, I . . .

LOTTIE. Listen, she's got a nice, big house here, hasn't she? She can take in roomers if she has to. And Mama left her two thousand dollars when she died, didn't she? Yes, Cora was the baby, so Mama left the money to her. I'm not going to worry.

REENIE. (*Upstairs L.*) Aunt Lottie!

MORRIS. All right. I was just wondering.

LOTTIE. Now remember. All you've got to say is, "I'm leaving all that to Lottie, Cora."

MORRIS. Yes, honey. (*Reenie comes down stairs looking somewhat wan and frightened)*

LOTTIE. Shhhh! (*Now she turns to Reenie with a prepared smile)* Well, Honey, aren't you getting ready for your party? Morris and I are dying to see your new dress.

REENIE. I don't feel well. I wish I didn't have to go.

LOTTIE. (*Alarmed*) You don't feel well? Did you tell your mother?

REENIE. Yes. But she won't believe me. I wish you'd tell her, Aunt Lottie.

LOTTIE. (*Rushes excitedly into dining room U.L.*) Cora! Reenie says she isn't feeling well. Cora, I think maybe she shouldn't go to the party. She says she doesn't want to go. Cora, what do you think is wrong?

CORA. (*Enters parlor from dining room—followed by Lottie)* There's nothing wrong with the child, Lottie.

LOTTIE. But she says she isn't feeling well, Cora. (*Turns to Reenie*) Come here, Honey, let me see if you've got a temperature. No. Not a sign of temperature. Stick out your tongue. Are you sick at your stomach?

REENIE. Kind of.

LOTTIE. My God, Cora. Her little hands are like ice.

CORA. (*Quite calm and wise*) There's nothing wrong with the child, Lottie. She gets to feeling like this every time she goes to a party.

34

LOTTIE. She's not going to have a very good time if she doesn't feel well.

CORA. It's something she's got to get over, Lottie. Plans are already made now. I got her the dress and she's got a date with a boy who's come here all the way from California. Now I'm not going to let her play sick and not go. The Ralston girl would never invite Reenie to another party as long as she lived if she backed out now. (*Her strategy defeated, Reenie goes back upstairs*)

LOTTIE. It's awful funny when a young girl doesn't want to go to a party, don't you think so, Morris? (*She watches Reenie's departure puzzledly*) I thought of something. I've got a bottle of perfume I'm going to give her. It's Coty's L'Origan. Finest perfume made. One of the big drug stores in Oklahoma City was having an anniversary sale. With each box of Coty's face powder, they gave you a little bottle of perfume, stuck right on top of the box. Morris, run out to the car and get me that package. It's on the back seat. I'll take it upstairs to Reenie. It'll make her feel good, don't you think?

CORA. That's very thoughtful of you, Lottie.

MORRIS. (*On his way to door R.*) You'll have her smelling like a fancy woman.

LOTTIE. (*With a sudden bite*) How do *you* know what a fancy woman smells like?

MORRIS. I can make a joke, can't I? (*Morris exits R. Cora and Lottie sit on either sides of table C.*)

LOTTIE. It was a wonderful dinner, Cora.

CORA. I'm glad you thought so. It all tasted like ashes to me.

LOTTIE. Oh, now, Cora, quit taking on.

CORA. Seventeen years we've been married, Lottie, and we still can't get along.

LOTTIE. What are you talking about? Why, I've known times when you got along just fine . . . for months at a time.

CORA. When Rubin was gone.

LOTTIE. Cora, that's not so.

CORA. Lottie, it's not good for kids to see their parents fighting.

LOTTIE. Cora, you've got the two nicest kids in the whole world. Why, they're wonderful children, Cora.

CORA. I worry about them, Lottie. . . . You saw Reenie just now.

35

Here she is sick, because she's going to a party, when most girls her age would be tickled to death. And the other boys tease Sonny so.

LOTTIE. Oh, Reenie'll get over that. So will Sonny.

CORA. Kids don't just "get over" these things, in some magic way. These troubles stay with kids sometimes, and affect their lives when they grow up.

MORRIS. (*Returns R. with a small package*) This what you want?

LOTTIE. Yes. Reenie—I've got something for you, Reenie. I've got something here to make you smell good. Real French perfume. Morris says it'll make you smell like a fancy woman. (*Goes running upstairs L, exuding her own brand of sudden warmth and affection*)

CORA. Lottie's awful good-hearted, Morris.

MORRIS. She thinks an awful lot of your kids, Cora.

CORA. I know she does. Morris, I've been thinking, wouldn't it be nice if Sonny and Reenie could go to those big schools you have in Oklahoma City. I mean . . .

LOTTIE. (*Hurrying back downstairs*) Cora, I wish you'd let me curl Reenie's hair for her. I could have her looking like a real baby doll. I'm an artist at it. Last week, Morris took me to a party at the Shrine, and everybody told me I had the prettiest head of hair at the whole party.

CORA. Go on and do it.

LOTTIE. I can't right now. She's in the bathtub. When are you going to get your hair bobbed, Cora?

CORA. Rubin doesn't like bobbed hair.

LOTTIE. Oh, he doesn't! You like my bobbed hair, don't you, Morris?

MORRIS. It's all right, honey.

LOTTIE. I'll be darned if I'd let any man tell me whether I could bob my hair or not. Why, I wouldn't go back to long hair now for anything. Morris says maybe I should take up smoking cigarettes now. Would you believe it, Cora? Women all over Oklahoma City are smoking cigarettes now. Isn't that disgraceful? What in God's name are we all coming to?

CORA. (*There is too much on her mind for her to partake now of Lottie's small talk*) I . . . I'd better finish up in the kitchen. (*Exits through parlor U.C. and into dining room*)

LOTTIE. Morris, I don't know what to do. I just can't bear to see little Cora so unhappy.

MORRIS. After all, it's not your worry, Honey.

LOTTIE. Oh, I know, but in a way it *is* my worry. I mean, I've always looked after Cora, ever since we were girls. I took her to her teacher the first day of school. I gave up the wishbone for her everytime we had fried chicken. She was the baby of the family, and I guess we all felt we had to pamper her.

MORRIS. Honey, if you want to take in her and the kids, it's up to you. We'd manage somehow.

LOTTIE. Oh God, Morris! Life's be miserable.

SONNY. (*Enters through parlor U.C.*) Wanta see my movie stars, Aunt Lottie?

LOTTIE. I guess so, honey. (*Sonny goes into parlor to get scrapbooks as Lottie turns to Morris with a private voice*) Every time we come over here we've got to look at his movie stars.

MORRIS. (*Lottie and Morris sat at table C.*) Got any of Norma Talmadge?

SONNY. (*Spreading the scrapbook on the floor before them*) Sure.

LOTTIE. Norma Talmadge, Norma Talmadge! That's all you ever think about is Norma Talmadge. I don't know what you see in her. Besides, she's a Catholic.

MORRIS. Honey, you've just got a bug about the Catholics.

LOTTIE. Oh I do, do I! Maybe you'd like to marry Norma Talmadge some day and then let the Pope tell you what to do the rest of your life, making you swear to leave all your money to the church, and bring up all your children Catholic, and then join the Knights of Columbus and take an oath to go out and kill all the nice Protestant women when the day comes for the Catholics to take over the world. (*Cora enters parlor U.C. now on way to sideboard, then wanders into the living room*)

MORRIS. Honey, where do you pick up these stories?

LOTTIE. Well, it's the truth. Marietta Flagmeyer told me. Cora, Marietta has this very close friend who used to be a Catholic but isn't any more. She even joined a convent, but she ran away because she found out all those things and wouldn't stand for them. This friend told Marietta that the Catholics keep the basements of their churches filled with guns and all kinds of ammunition . . .

37

CORA. (*She has heard Lottie's rantings before*) Lottie! (*She shakes her head hopelessly and returns to parlor U.C. on way to kitchen*)

LOTTIE. . . . because some day they plan to rise and take over the world, and kill off all the rest of us who don't want to be Catholics. I believe every word of it, too.

MORRIS. Well . . . I still like Norma Talmadge. Got any of Bebe Daniels?

SONNY. Yes. (*Hands Morris a picture which Lottie snaps up first for an approving look*)

LOTTIE. I don't know what you see in her. (*Now passes the picture on to Morris*)

MORRIS. You don't like any of the women stars, Honey.

LOTTIE. I guess I don't. I hear they're all a bunch of trollops. (*Now to Sonny*) Honey, when is your daddy coming home?

SONNY. Oh, he's not coming back at all. He and Mom had a fight. Here's one of your favorites, Aunt Lottie. (*He hands her a picture*)

LOTTIE. Who? Rudolph Valentino, he's not one of my favorites at all.

MORRIS. You saw "The Sheik" four times.

LOTTIE. That's just because Marietta Flagmeyer wanted me to keep her company.

MORRIS. Rudolph Valentino must be a Catholic too. He's an Eye-talian.

LOTTIE. But he's not a Catholic. Marietta's friend has a book that lists all the people in Hollywood who are Catholics. (*She studies the picture very intently*) You know, it scares me a little to look at him. Those eyes, that seem to be laughing at you, and all those white teeth. I think it's a sin for a man to be as pretty as he is. Why, I'd be scared to death to let a man like him touch me. (*Cora returns U.L. now without her apron. She is carrying a paper bag*) But you know, they say he's really a very nice man. Cora, do you know there's this woman over in Oklahoma City who worships Rudolph Valentino. That's the truth. Marietta knows her. She's made a little shrine to him down in her basement, and she keeps the room filled with candles and she goes down there every day and says a little prayer for him.

CORA. I thought you were going to fix Reenie's hair.

LOTTIE. Oh, yes. I guess she's out of the bathtub now.

CORA. (*Puts the sack on the table*) There's a lot of fried chicken left, Lottie. I brought you some to take home with you.

LOTTIE. Won't you and the kids want it?

CORA. They won't eat anything but the breast.

LOTTIE. Thanks, Cora.

CORA. Sonny, I don't want your pictures all over the floor when the young people come by for Reenie.

SONNY. All right.

MORRIS. (*As Lottie takes a drumstick out of the sack*) Honey, you just ate.

LOTTIE. Don't scold me, Daddy. (*Now she whispers boldly to him before starting upstairs*) Remember what I told you, Morris. (*Now she goes hurrying upstairs L.*) Reenie! I'm coming up to fix your hair. I'm going to turn you into a real baby doll.

REENIE. (*Upstairs L.*) I'm in here, Aunt Lottie. (*Lottie off*) (*Morris draws over to the door as though hoping to evade Cora*)

CORA. Morris . . . Morris! I suppose Lottie told you what's happened.

MORRIS. Well, uh . . . yes, Cora . . . she said something about it.

CORA. I guess now that maybe my folks were right, Morris. I shouldn't have married Rubin.

MORRIS. You're going to forget all this squabble after a while, Cora. So's Rubin.

CORA. I don't think we *should* forget it. I don't think we should *try* to come back together. I think I've failed.

MORRIS. Now Cora, I think you're exaggerating things in your own mind.

CORA. Morris, I'm only thirty-four. That's still young. I thought I'd like to take the kids to Oklahoma City and put them in school there, and get myself a job in one of the department stores. I know I've never done work like that, but I think I'd like it, and . . . it seems to me that I've got to, Morris, I've got to.

MORRIS. Well, Cora . . . maybe . . .

LOTTIE. (*Upstairs L.*) Let's go into the bathroom, Reenie, where the light's better.

MORRIS. It's awful hard, Cora, being on your feet all day.

CORA. But I'd get used to it.

MORRIS. Well . . . it's hard for me to advise you, Cora.

CORA. Morris, I was wondering if maybe the kids and I could come and live with you and Lottie for a while. Just for a while. Until we got used to the city. Until I got myself a job and we felt more or less at home.

MORRIS. Well, I . . . uh . . .

CORA. I promise we wouldn't be any bother. I mean, I'd keep things straightened up after the kids, and do as much of the cooking as Lottie wanted me to do.

MORRIS. Well, I . . . uh . . .

CORA. I just don't know what else the kids and I can do, Morris.

MORRIS. Yes. Well . . . Cora, I don't know just what to say.

CORA. Would we be too much in the way, Morris?

MORRIS. Oh no. Of course not, Cora. *But . . .*

CORA. (*Hopefully*) I think we could manage. And I'd pay our share of the bills. I'd insist on that. (*Flirt, Punky and Sammy are seen through the window coming onto porch C.R.*)

MORRIS. Well, Cora, I . . .

LOTTIE. (*Comes hurtling halfway down the stairs, full of anxiety*) Cora, Reenie's sick. She's vomiting all over the bathroom. (*She bustles back upstairs as Cora starts to follow*)   DOORBELL RINGS

CORA. Oh, my God! (*Now the doorbell rings R., catching Cora for a moment*) Oh dear! It's the young people after Reenie. Sonny, put on your manners and answer the door. (*Sonny runs to the door R., turning on porch light before opening it, and we see the three young people on the porch outside, Flirt in dazzling party dress, and the two boys in uniforms from a nearby military academy. One boy, Punky Givens, is seen drinking from a flask, preparing himself to meet people. Inside, Cora starts upstairs in worried concern*) Oh dear! What could be wrong with the child? Morris, try to entertain the young people until I get back. (*Cora off L. Sonny swings open the door*)

SONNY. Won't you come in?

FLIRT. (*Comes dancing into the hallway, bringing the atmosphere of a chilly spring night with her*) Hi, Sonny! Is your sister ready?

SONNY. Not yet.

FLIRT. Oh shucks! (*Sticks her head out the door*) Come on in, fellows. We're going to have to wait. (*Punky Givens and*

Sammy Goldenbaum make a colorful entrance. Both are dressed in uniforms of lustrous blue which fit them like smooth upholstery. Flirt commences the introductions) Sammy, this is Sonny Flood, Reenie's little brother. *(Sammy Goldenbaum steps forth correctly, his plumed headgear in his hand. He is a darkly beautiful young man of seventeen, with lustrous black hair, black eyes and a captivating smile. Yet, there seems something a little foreign about him at least in comparison with the Midwestern company in which he now finds himself. He could be a Persian prince, strayed from his native kingdom. But he has become adept over the years in adapting himself, and he shows an eagerness to make friends and to be liked)*

SAMMY. Hi, Sonny!

SONNY. *(Shaking hands)* Hi!

FLIRT. *(Bringing him up from the rear)* And this is Punky Givens. *(She all but drags Punky from the dark corner of the hallway to face the lighted room full of people. For Punky is a disappointment as a human being. The military academy as yet has done nothing for his posture, and he wears his uniform as though embarrassed by its splendour. He offers a limp hand when being introduced, mumbles some incoherent greeting, and then retires in hopes that no one will notice him. These introductions made, Flirt now notices Morris)* Oh, hello! I'm Flirt Conroy. How're you?

MORRIS. How d'ya do? I'm Morris Lacey. Reenie's uncle. From Oklahoma City.

FLIRT. Oh yes, I've heard her speak about you. Fellows, this is Dr. Lacey. He's Reenie's uncle. From Oklahoma City.

SAMMY. *(Crossing the room to present himself to Morris, he is brisk and alert, even though his speech betrays a slight stammer)* How do you do, Sir? My name is G-Goldenbaum. Sammy, they call me.

MORRIS. Glad to know you, Sammy.

FLIRT. And this is Punky Givens. *(Nudging him)* Stand up straight, Punky.

MORRIS. Glad to know you, Punky. *(Punky mumbles. Morris now feels the burden of his responsibility as temporary host)* Uh . . . anyone care for a Life Saver? *(He offers a pack from his pocket, but no one is interested. Now Lottie comes bustling down the stairs, eager to take over the situation, babbling all the way down of exuberant inconsequentials)*

LOTTIE. Hello, everyone! I'm Lottie Lacey, Reenie's aunt. I'm Cora Flood's sister. From Oklahoma City. Oklahoma City's a great big town now. People say in another ten years, it's going to be the biggest city in the whole United States, bigger even than New York or Chicago. You're the little Conroy girl, aren't you? I've heard my sister speak of you. My! What a pretty red dress. Have you all met my husband? Dr. Lacey. He's a dentist. Come over to Oklahoma City and he'll pull all your teeth. *(She laughs heartily and then her eyes slowly widen at the magnificent uniforms)* My goodness! Aren't those handsome get-ups?

SAMMY. *(Stepping forth)* How do you do Ma'am? I'm Sammy Goldenbaum. From California.

LOTTIE. Oh yes. Cora told me about the young man from California. He's from Hollywood, Morris. His mother's in the movies. Has she played in anything I might have seen?

SAMMY. She was in T-Thomas Meighan's last picture. Her name is Gertrude Vanderhof. It was a very small part. She isn't a star or anything.

LOTTIE. Gertrude Vanderhof! Did we see Thomas Meighan's last picture, Morris? I don't believe so. I like Thomas Meighan but we don't have time to see *all* the movies. Do you think you ever saw Gertrude Vanderhof in anything, Morris? *(Lottie seems to refer to her husband on every topic without waiting for his judgment. Nevertheless, Morris mulls this last query over as Flirt interrupts)*

FLIRT. Mrs. Lacey, have you met Punky Givens?

LOTTIE. How do you do? I've heard my sister speak of you. Your people are very prominent in town, aren't they? Yes, I've heard Cora speak of them. *(Punky offers a hand and mumbles)* What did you say? *(He repeats his mumble. Lottie is still at sea but makes the best of things)* Thank you very much. *(At the top of the stairs, we see Reenie's feet trying to get up the courage to bring her down, and we hear Cora coaxing her)*

CORA. *(Off L.)* Go on, Reenie. *(But Reenie can't make it yet. The feet go scurrying back to safety)*

42

LOTTIE. (*Trying to avoid embarrassment*) Well, I'm afraid you're all going to have to wait a few minutes. Reenie isn't quite ready.

CORA. (*Upstairs L.*) Reenie, not another word.

LOTTIE. Cora's upstairs now helping her. I guess you'll have to entertain yourselves a while. Do any of you play Mah Jong? (*Notices the sack of fried chicken and hides it under the table*)

FLIRT. I want to play some music. Got any new piano rolls, Sonny?

SONNY. A few. (*They run into the parlor U.C. to the piano*)

FLIRT. Gee, I wish you had a Victrola like we do.

LOTTIE. (*Sitting C., turning her attention to Sammy*) My, you're a long way from home, aren't you?

SAMMY. Yes, Ma'am. (*Morris crosses D.L. Sits in leather armchair*)

LOTTIE. Morris and I went to California once. A Shriner's convention. Oh, we thought it was perfectly wonderful, all those oranges and things. Didn't we, Morris? I should think you'd want to go home on your spring vacation.

SAMMY. Well, I . . . I guess I don't really have a home . . . Mrs. Lacey. (*Sonny wanders back from the parlor. Sammy fills him with curiosity and fascination*)

LOTTIE. Did you tell me your mother lived out there?

SAMMY. Yes, but you see, she's pretty busy in moving pictures, and . . . Oh, she feels awfully bad that she doesn't have more time for me. Really she does. But she doesn't have a place where I could stay right now . . . and . . . But, it's not *her* fault.

LOTTIE. Where's your father?

SAMMY. Oh, I never knew him.

LOTTIE. You never knew your father?

SAMMY. No. You see, he died before I was born. My mother has been married . . . a few times since then. But I never met any of her husbands . . . although they were all very fine gentlemen.

LOTTIE. Well—I just never knew anyone who didn't have a home. Do you spend your whole life in military academies?

SAMMY. Just about. I bet I've been in almost every military academy in the whole country. Well, I take that back. There's some I didn't go to. I mean . . . there's some that wouldn't take me.

43

SONNY. (*Out of the innocent blue*) My mother says you're a Jew.

LOTTIE. (*Aghast*) Sonny!

SAMMY. Well . . . yes, Sonny. I guess I am.

LOTTIE. (*Consolingly*) That's perfectly all right. Why, we don't think a thing about a person's being Jewish, do we, Morris?

MORRIS. No. Of course not.

SAMMY. My father was Jewish. Mother told me. Mother isn't Jewish at all. Oh, my mother has the most beautiful blond hair. I guess I take after my father . . . in looks, anyhow. He was an actor, too, but he got killed in an automobile accident.

LOTTIE. That's too bad. Sonny, I think you should apologize.

SONNY. Did I say something bad?

SAMMY. Oh, that's all right. It doesn't bother me that I'm Jewish. Not any more. I guess it used to a little. . . . Yes, it did used to a little.

LOTTIE. (*Who must find a remedy for everything*) You know what you ought to do? You ought to join the Christian Science Church. Now I'm not a member myself, but I know this Jewish woman over in Oklahoma City, and she was very, very unhappy, wasn't she, Morris? But she joined the Christian Science Church and has been perfectly happy ever since.

SONNY. I didn't mean to say anything wrong.

SAMMY. You didn't say anything wrong, Sonny. (*The piano begins playing with precise, automatic rhythm. Flirt dances in from the parlor*)

FLIRT. Come on, Punky, let's dance. (*She sings*) "The Sheik of Araby—boom—boom—boom—his heart belongs to me." Come *on*, Punky.

SAMMY. (*To Lottie, always courteous*) Would you care to dance, Ma'am?

LOTTIE. Me? Good heavens no. I haven't danced since I was a girl. But I certainly appreciate your asking. Isn't he respectful, Morris? (*Lottie exits to dining room U.L.*)

SAMMY. Wanta wild west ride, Sonny? (*He kneels on the floor, permitting Sonny to straddle his back. Then Sammy kicks his feet in the air like a wild colt, as Sonny holds to him tight*)

FLIRT. (*At the back of the room U.C., instructs Punky in the intricacies of a new step*) No, Punky. That's not it. You take one

44

step to the left and then *dip*. See? Oh, it's a wonderful step, and all the kids are doing it.

LOTTIE. (*Enters from kitchen U.L. with a plate of cookies which she offers Sammy and Sonny*) Would you like a cookie?

SAMMY. (*Getting to his feet, the ride over*) Gee, that gets to be pretty strenuous. (*Flirt and Punky now retire to the parlor U.C. where they indulge in a little private petting*)

SONNY. Where did you get those clothes?

SAMMY. They gave them to me at the academy, Sonny.

FLIRT. (*In the parlor, protesting Punky's advances.* Punky, *don't.* (*Lottie observes this little intimacy, having just started into parlor with the plate of cookies. It rouses some of her righteousness*)

SAMMY. No. I take that back. They didn't *give* them to me. They never give you anything at that place. I paid for them. Plenty!

SONNY. Why do you wear a sword?

SAMMY. (*Pulls the sword from its sheath like a buccaneer and goes charging about the room in search of imagined villains*) I wear a sword to protect myself! See! To kill off all the villains in the world. (*He frightens Lottie*) Oh, don't worry, Ma'am. It's not sharp. I couldn't hurt anyone with it, even if I wanted to. We just wear them for show.

SONNY. (*Jumping up and down*) Can I have a sword? I want a sword.

SAMMY. Do you, Sonny? Do you want a sword. Here, Sonny, I'll give you *my* sword, for all the good it'll do you.

LOTTIE. (*To Morris*) Cora will probably buy Sonny a sword now. (*Now Sammy takes the sword and imitates the actions of Sammy. Lottie is apprehensive*) Now you be careful, Sonny.

SAMMY. What do you want a sword for, Sonny?

SONNY. (*With a lunge*) To *show* people.

LOTTIE. Sonny! Be careful with that thing.

SAMMY. And what do you want to show people, Sonny?

SONNY. I just want to *show* 'em. (*He places the sword between his arm and his chest, then drops to the floor, the sword rising far above his body, giving the appearance that he is impaled. Lottie is horrified*)

LOTTIE. Oh darling—put it down. Sonny, please don't play with that nasty thing any more. (*Sonny rises now and laughs with*

45

Sammy. Lottie puts the sword away in the parlor where she again detects Flirt and Punky, now engaged in more serious necking. Morally outraged, she runs up the stairs to inform Cora)

SAMMY. *(Kneeling beside Sonny)* What'll we do now, Sonny? Are there any games you want to play? Do you want to fight Indians? or set bear traps? or go flying over volcanoes? or climb the Alps?

SONNY. *(Eagerly)* Yes . . . yes.

SAMMY. Gee, so do I, Sonny. But we can't. Not tonight anyway. What else can we do?

SONNY. I can show you my movie stars.

SAMMY. I've had enough of movie stars. What else?

SONNY. I can speak a piece.

SAMMY. You can? *(Jumps to his feet)* Hey, everyone! Stop the music. Sonny's going to speak a piece. *(Sammy stops the piano, giving Flirt some annoyance)*

LOTTIE. *(Hurrying downstairs)* Did you hear that, Morris? Sonny's going to speak a piece.

FLIRT. *(To Sammy)* Hey, what are you doing?

SAMMY. *(To Sonny)* Where do you want to stand, sir?

LOTTIE. He's got a little platform in the parlor where he practices.

SAMMY. *(Having taken over like an impresario)* Into the parlor, everyone. Into the parlor to hear Sonny speak his piece.

FLIRT. *(Pulling Punky's arm)* Come on, Punky. Come on. We *have* to listen, don't we?

SAMMY. Quiet everyone. Quiet! *(All enter the parlor but Morris, who crosses R. as Sonny begins the famous soliloquy. Morris looks as though he might share some of Hamlet's woes. After Sonny begins, Cora starts down the stairs with Reenie. Morris stands far R.)*

SONNY.

> To be or not to be, that is the question
> Whether tis nobler in the mind to suffer
> The slings and arrows of outrageous fortune
> Or to take arms against a sea of troubles,
> And by opposing end them.
> To die: to sleep:
> No more; and, by a sleep to say we end the heartache and

46

the thousand natural shocks that flesh is heir to, 'tis a
consumption devoutly to be wish'd.
To die, to sleep; To sleep; perchance to dream.
Ay, there's the rub,
For in that sleep of death what dreams may come when we
have shuffled off this mortal coil, Must give us pause.
(*There is immediate loud acclaim for Sonny*)
CORA. Oh, Sonny's reciting. Why, he's reciting Shakespeare. He
must have gotten out that dusty volume of Shakespeare over in the
bookcase, and memorized that speech all on his own. (*Points to
Sammy in the parlor*) Reenie, there's your young man. Isn't he
handsome? Now you're going to have a good time. I can feel it in
my bones.
SAMMY. That was *wonderful*, Sonny. (*All come from parlor now,
Sammy carrying Sonny on his shoulders like a triumphant hero*)
LOTTIE. He's a second Jackie Coogan.
FLIRT. That was just wonderful, Sonny.
LOTTIE. Cora, you should have been here. Sonny recited Shake-
speare. It was just wonderful.
CORA. Yes. I heard him.
SAMMY. Sonny's a genius. I'm going to take you to Hollywood,
Sonny, and put you in the movies. You'll be the greatest actor out
there, Sonny.
FLIRT. Oh, I think Shakespeare's just wonderful. I'm going to
read him sometime, really I am.
CORA. (*Going to Sammy*) Good evening, young man. I'm Mrs.
Flood.
SAMMY. (*Putting Sonny down*) Beg your pardon, Ma'am. I'm
Sammy Goldenbaum.
CORA. Welcome. I see my son's been entertaining you.
SAMMY. He sure has, Ma'am.
CORA. He started speaking pieces about a year ago. Just picked
it up. Some people think he's talented.
SAMMY. I think so, too, Ma'am. Very.
CORA. (*Bring Reenie forth*) Reenie! Sammy, this is my daughter
Reenie.
SAMMY. Good evening, Reenie.
REENIE. (*Reluctantly*) Good evening.

47

SAMMY. You certainly look nice. That's a very beautiful dress.

FLIRT. Isn't it cute! I helped her pick it out. (*Cora quietly takes hold of Flirt's arm and prevents her from taking over*) Ouch!

SAMMY. Gee! I didn't expect you to be . . . like you are. L mean . . . well, Punky told me you were a friend of Flirt's so I just naturally thought you'd be . . . well, kind of like Flirt is. Although Flirt is a very nice girl. I didn't mean to imply anything against her. But . . . *you're* very nice, too, in a different way.

REENIE. (*Still a little distrustful*) Thank you . . .

SAMMY. Would you call me *Sammy?*

REENIE. Sammy.

SAMMY. And may I call you Reenie?

REENIE. I guess so.

SAMMY. It's awfully nice of you to let me take you to the party. I know just how a girl feels, going out with some crazy guy she doesn't even know.

REENIE. Oh . . . that's all right. After all, you don't know anything about me, either.

SAMMY. You know, I've never been to many parties, have you?

REENIE. Not many.

SAMMY. I always worry that maybe people aren't going to like me when I go to a party. Isn't that crazy? Do you ever get kind of a sick feeling in the pit of your stomach when you dread things? Gee, I wouldn't want to miss a party for anything. But every time I go to one, I have to reason with myself to keep from feeling that the whole world's against me. See, I've spent almost my whole life in military academies. My mother doesn't have a place for me, where she lives. She . . . she just doesn't know what else to do with me. But you mustn't misunderstand about my mother. She's really a very lovely person. I guess every boy thinks his mother is very beautiful, but my mother really is. She tells me in every letter she writes how sorry she is that we can't be together more, but she has to think of her work. One time we were together, though. She met me in San Francisco once, and we were together for two whole days. Just like we were sweethearts. It was the most wonderful time I ever had. And then I had to go back to the old military academy. Every time I walk into the barracks, I get kind of a depressed feeling. It's got hard stone walls. Pictures of generals

hanging all over . . . oh, they're very fine gentlemen, but they all look so kind of hard-boiled and stern . . . you know what I mean. (*Cora and Lottie stand together, listening to Sammy's speech with motherly expressions. Flirt is bored, Punky is half asleep, and gives now a sudden, audible yawn that startles everyone*) Well, gee! I guess I've bored you enough, telling you about myself.
CORA and LOTTIE. Oh, no. You haven't either.
FLIRT. (*Impatient to get to the party*) Come on, kids. Let's hurry.
SAMMY. (*Tenderly to Reenie*) Are you ready?
CORA. (*As though fearing Reenie might bolt and run*) Reenie?
REENIE. Yes.
SAMMY. May I help you into your wrap? (*The word* wrap *is a false glorification of her Sunday coat, which he offers her, helping her into it*)
REENIE. Thank you.
CORA. (*Whispering to Lottie*) I wish I could have bought her one of those little fur jackets like Flirt is wearing.
FLIRT. Stand up straight, Punky, and say good night to everyone. (*Punky tries again, but remains inarticulate*)
CORA. (*Assuming that Punky said good night*) Good night, Punky. Tell your mother hello for me.
FLIRT. Very pleased to have met you, Mr. and Mrs. Lacey. Good night, Mrs. Flood.
CORA. Good night, Flirt.
LOTTIE and MORRIS. Good night.
SONNY. (*Pulling at Sammy's coat tails*) Do you have to go?
SAMMY. I'm afraid I do, Sonny.
SONNY. Can I go, too? Please? Can I go, too?
SAMMY. Gee, I don't know. (*He thinks a moment and then consults Flirt and Punky*) Hey, is there any reason Sonny can't come along? I promise to look after him. Think what a great time he'd have. (*Flirt and Punky look dubious*)
SONNY. (*Takes his welcome immediately for granted and dances about the room joyously*) Goody, goody! I'm going to the party. I'm going to the party.
REENIE. (*Running to Cora's side*) Mother, I'm not going if Sonny goes, too. Other girls don't have to be bothered by their little brothers.

49

CORA. I agree with you, Daughter.

FLIRT. No. It's not a kids' party, Sammy. That was a stupid idea. I think you should mind your own business.

CORA. (*Trying to cool Flirt's temper*) Now, Flirt.

FLIRT. (*To Reenie*) He's always trying to boss everyone.

CORA. (*To Sammy*) I guess Sonny'd better not go.

SONNY. (*Crying, jumping in protest*) I want to go to the party. I want to go to the party.

SAMMY. (*Trying to be consoling*) I guess it was a pretty dumb idea, Sonny.

SONNY. I WANT TO GO TO THE PARTY! I WANT TO GO TO THE PARTY! (*Sonny flies into a real tantrum now, throws himself on the floor, pounding the floor with his fists and kicking it with his toes, his face red with rage. Cora and Lottie flutter about him like nervous hens*)

CORA. Sonny! Sonny! Stop it this instant. Sonny, I'll not let you go to another movie for a whole month if you don't stop.

LOTTIE. Oh, what'll I do? Oh, here, Sonny, do you want a little cookie, sweetheart?

FLIRT. Now we'll never get there.

CORA. I never can do a thing with him when he throws one of these tantrums.

SAMMY. (*Quietly goes to Sonny's side and speaks in a voice that is firm with authority, yet still thoughtful and considerate*) Sonny, that's no way to behave.

SONNY. (*Suddenly quiet*) Isn't it?

SAMMY. No, Sonny. You mustn't ever act like that.

SONNY. (*More reasonable now*) But I want to go to the party.

SAMMY. But if you act that way, no one's *ever* going to ask you to a party.

SONNY. Aren't they?

SAMMY. No, Sonny. You have to be a good boy before people ask you to parties. Even then, they don't always ask you.

SONNY. I love parties more than anything else in the world.

SAMMY. So do I, Sonny. I love parties, too. But there's lots of parties I can't go to.

SONNY. Honest?

SAMMY. Honest. It was wrong of me to suggest that you go to

50

the party tonight. You're not old enough yet. You'll be old enough some day though and then you can go to all the parties you like.

SONNY. Can I?

SAMMY. Sure. Now, I tell you what I'll go. I'll gather up all the favors I can find at the party. Want me to? And I'll give them to your sister to bring home to you. And then you can have a party here all by yourself. Would you like that? You can throw a big party in Sammy's honor, without any old grownups around to interfere. Will that make you happy?

SONNY. Yes, yes.

SAMMY. O.K. Are we still buddies?

SONNY. Yes.

SAMMY. Forever and ever?

SONNY. Forever and ever. (*Sonny hugs him impulsively*)

SAMMY. Gee! I love kids.

CORA. (*Awed as though by a miracle*) You're the first person in the entire world who's ever been able to do a thing with the boy when he goes into one of his tantrums.

SAMMY. You know, it's funny, but . . . I always seem to know just how kids feel.

FLIRT. (*Still impatient*) Come on, Sammy. (*Flirt and Punky exit R.*)

CORA. Good night, Sammy. I hope you'll be able to come back sometime.

SAMMY. Thank you, Ma'am. It's very nice to feel welcome.

LOTTIE and MORRIS. Good night. Come over to see us sometime in Oklahoma City. It's a big town. You can stay in the extra bedroom. I hope you like cats.

CORA. Oh, Reenie, don't forget your present. You're feeling better now, aren't you?

REENIE. Yes, Mom.

SAMMY. (*Breaking away from Lottie and Morris*) Excuse me. (*Sammy offers Reenie his arm now and they walk proudly out together*)

CORA. (*After the exit*) Why, that's the nicest young man I ever met.

LOTTIE. I thought so too, Cora. And my goodness, he was handsome. Morris says he felt sorry for him, though. (*Sonny exits to Dining Room U.L.*)

CORA. (*Sitting at table C.*) Sorry? Oh, Morris.

LOTTIE. He seemed like a perfectly happy boy to me. But Morris says he looked like a very unhappy boy to him. What makes you think that, Morris?

MORRIS. (*Returning to chair D.L.*) Oh . . . I don't know.

CORA. Unhappy? Why, he made himself right at home, didn't he?

LOTTIE. I should say he did. He was laughing and enjoying himself. But Morris says sometimes the people who act the happiest are really the saddest.

CORA. Oh, Morris.

LOTTIE. Morris, I think you make these things up. Ever since you went to that psychologist, you've gone around imagining everyone's unhappy. (*Morris quietly gets up and walks ao the door R., leaving Lottie to wonder if she has said anything wrong*) Where are you going, Morris?

MORRIS. Thought I'd go out for a little walk, Honey. (*Morris exits*)

LOTTIE. (*Following him to the door*) Oh. Well, don't be gone long. We've got to get started back soon.

CORA. Oh, please don't talk about going.

LOTTIE. My God, Cora, we can't stay here all night. (*She peers out the window now, wondering about Morris*) Morris is funny, Cora. Sometimes he just gets up like that and walks away. I never know why. Sometimes he's gone for hours at a time. He says the walk helps his digestion, but I think it's because he just wants to get away from me at times. Did you ever notice how he is with people? Like tonight. He sat there when all the young people were here, and he didn't say hardly a word. His mind was a thousand miles away. Like he was thinking about something. He seems to be always thinking about something.

CORA. Morris is nice to you. You've got no right to complain.

LOTTIE. (*Joining Cora at table C.*) He's nice to me . . . in *some* ways.

CORA. Good heavens, Lottie! He gave you those red patent leather slippers, and that fox neckpiece . . . you should be grateful.

LOTTIE. I know, but . . . there's *some* things he hasn't given me.

52

CORA. Lottie! That's not his fault. You've got no right to hold that against him!

LOTTIE. Oh, it's just fine for you to talk. You've got two nice kids to keep you company. What have I got but a house full of cats.

CORA. Lottie, you always claimed you never wanted children.

LOTTIE. Well . . . what else can I say to people?

CORA. (*This is something of a revelation to her*) I just never knew.

LOTTIE. (*Having suddenly decided to say it*) Cora . . . I can't let you and the kids come over and live with us.

CORA. (*This is a blow to her*) Oh . . . Lottie.

LOTTIE. I'm sorry, Cora. I just can't do it.

CORA. Lottie, I was depending on you. . . .

LOTTIE. Maybe you've depended on me too much. Ever since you were a baby, you've run to me with your problems, and now I've got problems of my own.

CORA. What am I going to do, Lottie?

LOTTIE. Call up Rubin and ask him to come back. Beg him to come back, if you have to get down on your knees.

CORA. I mustn't do that, Lottie.

LOTTIE. Why not?

CORA. Because we just can't keep from fighting, Lottie. You know that. I just don't think it's right, our still going on that way.

LOTTIE. Do you still love him?

CORA. Oh . . . don't ask me, Lottie.

LOTTIE. Do you?

CORA. Oh . . . yes.

LOTTIE. Cora, I don't think you should listen to the stories those old Werpel sisters tell you.

CORA. He's as good as admitted it, Lottie.

LOTTIE. Well, Cora, I don't think it means he likes you any the less, because he's seen Mavis Pruitt a few times.

CORA. No. . . . I know he loves me.

LOTTIE. (*Asking very cautiously*) Does he still want to be intimate?

CORA. That's only animal, Lottie. I couldn't indulge myself that way if I didn't feel he was being honorable.

LOTTIE. (*Breaks into a sudden raucous laugh*) My God, a big, handsome buck like Rubin! Who cares if he's honorable?

CORA. (*A little shocked*) Lottie!

LOTTIE. (*We see now a sudden lewdness in Lottie that has not been discernible before*) Cora, did you hear what the Old Maid said to the burglar? You see, the burglar came walking into her bedroom with this big, long billy club and . . .

CORA. Lottie!

LOTTIE. (*Laughing so hard she can hardly finish the story*) And the old maid . . . she was so green she didn't know what was happening to her, she said. . . .

CORA. Lottie! That's enough. That's enough.

LOTTIE. (*Shamed now*) Shucks, Cora. I don't see what's wrong in having a little fun just telling stories.

CORA. Sometimes you talk shamefully, Lottie, and when I think of the way Mama and Papa brought us up. . . .

LOTTIE. Oh, Mama and Papa, Mama and Papa! Maybe they didn't know as much as we gave them credit for.

CORA. You're changed since you were a girl, Lottie.

LOTTIE. What if I am!

CORA. I never heard such talk.

LOTTIE. Well, that's all it is. It's only talk. Talk, talk, talk.

CORA. Lottie, are you sure you can't take us in?

LOTTIE. It'd mean the end of my marriage too, Cora. You don't understand Morris. He's always nice and quiet around people, so afraid of hurting people's feelings. But he's the most nervous man around the house you ever saw. He'd try to make the best of it if you and the kids came over, but he'd go to pieces. I know he would.

CORA. Honest?

LOTTIE. I'm not joking, Cora. My God, you're not the only one who has problems. Don't think that for a minute.

CORA. A few moments ago, you said *you* had problems, Lottie. . . .

LOTTIE. Problems enough.

CORA. Tell me, Lottie.

LOTTIE. Oh, why should I?

CORA. Doesn't Morris ever make love to you any more?

LOTTIE. (*It takes her several moments to admit it*) . . . No. It's been over three years since he even touched me . . . that way.

CORA. (*Another revelation*) Lottie!

LOTTIE. It's the God's truth, Cora.

CORA. Lottie! What's wrong?

LOTTIE. How do I know what's wrong? How does anyone ever know what's wrong with anyone else?

CORA. I mean . . . is there another woman?

LOTTIE. Not unless she visits him from the spirit world. (*This releases her humor again and she is diverted by another story*) Oh, say, Cora, did I tell you about this woman over in Oklahoma City who's been holding seances? Well, Marietta went to her and. . . . (*But suddenly again, she loses her humor and makes another sad admission*) Oh, no, there isn't another woman. Sometimes I wish there was.

CORA. Lottie, you don't mean that.

LOTTIE. How the hell do *you* know what I mean? He's around the house all day long, now that he's got his dental office in the dining room. Day and night, day and night. Sometimes I get tired of looking at him.

CORA. Oh Lottie . . . I'd always felt you and Morris were so devoted to each other. I've always felt you had an almost perfect marriage.

LOTTIE. Oh, we're still devoted, still call each other 'honey' just like we did on our honeymoon.

CORA. But what happened? Something must have happened to . . .

LOTTIE. Did you notice the way Morris got up out of his chair suddenly and just walked away, with no explanation at all? Well, something inside Morris did the same thing several years ago. Something inside him just got up and went for a walk, and never came back.

CORA. I . . . just don't understand.

LOTTIE. Sometimes I wonder if maybe I've been too bossy. Could be. But then, I always supposed that Morris *liked* me because I was bossy.

CORA. I always envied you, having a husband you could boss.

LOTTIE. Yes, I can boss Morris because he just isn't there any more to fight back. He doesn't care any more if I boss him or not.

CORA. Just the same, he never hit you.

LOTTIE. I wish he would.

CORA. Lottie!

LOTTIE. I do. I wish to God someone *loved* me enough to hit me.

55

You and Rubin fight. Oh, God I'd like a good fight. Anything'd be better than this *nothing*. Morris and I go around always being so sweet to each other, but sometimes I wonder maybe he'd like to kill me.

CORA. Lottie, you don't mean it.

LOTTIE. Do you remember how Mama and Papa used to caution us about men, Cora?

CORA. Yes I remember.

LOTTIE. My God, they had me so afraid of ever giving in to a man, I was petrified.

CORA. So was I.

LOTTIE. Yes, you were until Rubin came along and practically raped you.

CORA. Lottie! I don't want Sonny to hear talk like that.

LOTTIE. Why not? Let him hear!

CORA. (*Newly aghast at her sister's boldness*) Lottie!

LOTTIE. Why do we feel we always have to protect kids?

CORA. Keep your voice down. Rubin never did anything like that.

LOTTIE. Didn't he?

CORA. Of course not!

LOTTIE. My God, Cora, he had you pregnant inside of two weeks after he started seeing you.

CORA. Sssh.

LOTTIE. I never told. I never even told Morris. My God, do you remember how Mama and Papa carried on when they found out?

CORA. I remember.

LOTTIE. And Papa had his stroke just a month after you were married. Oh, I just thought Rubin was the wickedest man alive.

CORA. I never blamed Rubin for that. I was crazy in love with him. He just swept me off my feet and made all my objections seem kinda silly. He even made Mama and Papa seem silly.

LOTTIE. Maybe I shoulda married a man like that. I don't know. Maybe it was as much my fault as Morris's. Maybe I didn't . . . respond right from the very first.

CORA. What do you mean, Lottie?

LOTTIE. Cora, I'll tell you something. Something I've never told another living soul. I never did enjoy it the way some women . . . say they do.

CORA. Lottie? You?

LOTTIE. Why do you say *me* like that? Because I talk kinda dirty at times? But that's all it is, is talk. I talk all the time just to convince myself that I'm alive. And I stuff myself with victuals just to feel I've got something inside me. And I'm full of all kinds of crazy curiosity about . . . all the things in life I seem to have missed out on. Now I'm telling you the truth, Cora. Nothing ever really happened to me while it was going on.

CORA. Lottie . . .

LOTTIE. That first night Morris and I were together, right after we were married, when we were in bed together for the first time, after it was all over, and he had fallen asleep, I lay there in bed wondering what in the world all the cautioning had been about. Nothing had happened to me at all, and I thought Mama and Papa musta been makin' things up.

CORA. Oh, Lottie!

LOTTIE. So, don't come to me for sympathy, Cora. I'm not the person to give it to you. (*Outside there is a low rumble of thunder. Sonny enters from the dining room U.L. with a cup of flour paste and his scrapbook. Morris returns from his walk R., his face mysterious and grave*)

MORRIS. We'd better be starting back now, Honey. It looks like rain.

CORA. Oh, don't talk about leaving. Can't you and Lottie stay all night? I'd get up early and fix you breakfast. I'll fix you biscuits.

MORRIS. I can't Cora. I got patients coming first thing in the morning.

LOTTIE. And I have to go home to let out the cats.

MORRIS. It was a wonderful dinner, Cora.

CORA. Thank you, Morris.

LOTTIE. (*On a sudden impulse, she springs to her feet, hoists her skirt to her waist, and begins wrestling with her corset*) My God, I'm gonna take off this corset and ride back home in comfort.

CORA. (*Runs protectively to Sonny, standing between him and Lottie to prevent his seeing this display*) Sonny! Turn your head.

LOTTIE. My God! That feels good. (*She rolls the corset under her arm and rubs the flesh on her stomach in appreciation of its new freedom. Then she reaches for the sack of fried chicken*)

Thanks for the fried chicken, Cora. Oh, good! A gizzard. (*She brings a gizzard out to gnaw on*) It was a wonderful dinner. You're a better cook than I am.

CORA. That's not so.

LOTTIE. Kiss me goodbye, Sonny.

SONNY. Goodbye, Aunt Lottie.

LOTTIE. (*Hugging him close*) Good night, darling.

MORRIS. That was a fine recitation, Edwin Booth.

SONNY. Thank you, Uncle Morris.

LOTTIE. (*Facing her husband now with a bright smile as though nothing but happiness had ever passed between them*) I'm ready, Daddy.

MORRIS. All right, Mama. Good of you to have us, Cora.

CORA. Glad you could come, Morris.

LOTTIE. (*At the door R., thinks of one last piece of news she must impart to her sister before leaving*) Oh Cora! I forgot to tell you. Mamie Keeler's in the hospital.

MORRIS. (*Goes out on the porch R. now*) Looks like it's gonna rain any minute now.

CORA. What's wrong?

LOTTIE. Some kind of female trouble.

CORA. Oh . . . that's too bad. (*But Lottie can tell by the sound of her voice that she is too preoccupied now with cares of her own to worry about Mamie Keeler*)

LOTTIE. Oh God, Cora . . . I just can't go off and leave you this way.

CORA. I'll be all right, Lottie.

LOTTIE. Look, Cora . . . if you and the kids wanta come over and stay with us . . . we'll manage somehow . . .

CORA. Oh, thank you, Lottie. (*They embrace as though recognizing the bond of their blood*) But I'm going to work this out for myself, Lottie.

LOTTIE. Goodbye, Cora.

MORRIS. (*From outside R.*) It's beginning to rain, Honey.

LOTTIE (*Hurrying out the door R.*) Hold your horses, Morris. I'm coming. Don't be impatient now. (*Off R. Now Cora returns C. feeling somehow deserted*)

SONNY. It's always so quiet after company leaves, isn't it?

CORA. Hush, Sonny. I'm trying to think. (*From outside R., we hear the sound of Morris's car driving off, and then the sound of the rain and the wind)*

SONNY. Let's move to California, Mom. Please, let's move to California. *(But Cora has made a sudden decision. She rushes to the telephone D.L.)*

CORA. Long Distance. *(A moment's wait)* This is Mrs. Flood at 321. I want to talk to Mr. Rubin Flood at the Hotel Boomerang in Blackwell . . . Yes, I'll wait.

SONNY. *(In an innocent voice)* I bet he isn't there. I bet anything.

CORA. Hello? He isn't? Would you ask them if he's been there this week? *(A moment's wait)* He hasn't! Oh . . . Well, please tell him, if he does come, to call his family immediately. It's very important. *(A fallen expression on her face, she sits for a moment, wondering what next move to make. Then she hears a car approach from the distance outside. She jumps up and runs to the window R.)*

SONNY. It isn't Dad. I can always tell the sound of his car. *(Cora returns C. now)*

CORA. Run along to bed now, Sonny. It's late. I have to go out and empty the pan under the ice-box. *(Cora goes out through the dining room door U.L. Sonny walks slowly, hesitantly to the foot of the stairs and stands there looking up at the blackness at the top. He stands there several moments, unable to force himself to go farther. From the kitchen we hear Cora's muffled cries. Sonny cries out in fear)*

SONNY. Mom! *(Cora returns now, not wanting Sonny to know she has been been crying)*

CORA. Sonny, I thought I told you to go upstairs. *(She looks at him now in his embarrassed fear)* Sonny, why are you so afraid of the dark?

SONNY. 'Cause . . . you can't see what's in front of you. And it might be something awful.

CORA. You're the man of the house now, Sonny. You mustn't be afraid.

SONNY. I'm not afraid . . . if someone's with me. *(Cora walks over to him and takes his hand)*

CORA. Come, boy. We'll go up together. *(They start up the stairs to face the darkness, hovering there like an omen)*

CURTAIN

ACT III

It is the next day, late afternoon. Outside, there is a drizzling rain that has continued through the day. Reenie has not dressed all day. She sits by the fire D.L. in her robe, rubbing her fresh shampooed hair with a towel. Cora enters from the dining room U.L., wearing a comfortable old kimona. She looks at the tray by Reenie's side.

CORA. Reenie! Is that all you feel like eating?

REENIE. Yes.

CORA. But that's all you've had all day, Reenie. You don't eat enough to keep a bird alive.

REENIE. I . . . I'm not hungry, Mom.

CORA. Now quit feeling sorry for yourself, just because you didn't have a good time last night.

REENIE. Mom, is Dad coming back?

CORA. I don't know. I tried to call him last night but couldn't get him.

REENIE. Aren't you mad at him any more?

CORA. No . . . I'm not mad.

REENIE. Even though he hit you?

CORA. Even though he hit me. I was defying him to do it . . . and he did. I can't blame him now.

REENIE. Do you think he *will* be back, Mom?

CORA. This is the day he was supposed to come back. It's almost supper time and he still isn't here.

REENIE. But it's been raining, Mom. I'll bet the roads are bad.

CORA. You love your father, don't you?

REENIE. Yes.

CORA. Well, I'm glad. The people we love aren't always perfect, are they? But if we love them, we have to take them as they are. After all, I guess I'm not perfect, either.

60

REENIE. You are too, Mom. You're absolutely perfect, in every way.

CORA. No, I'm not, Reenie. I . . . I have my own score to settle for. I've always accused your father of neglecting you kids, but maybe I've hurt you more with pampering. You . . . and Sonny, too.

REENIE. What do you mean, Mom?

CORA. Oh nothing. I can't say anything more about it right now. Forget it. (*For some reason she tries to change the subject*) Are you feeling a little better now?

REENIE. I guess so.

CORA. Well, the world isn't going to end just because your young man went off and left you.

REENIE. Oh, Mom. It was the most humiliating thing that ever happened to me.

CORA. Where do you think Sammy went?

REENIE. He went out to the cars at intermission time with some other girl.

CORA. To spoon?

REENIE. They call it *necking*.

CORA. Are you sure of this?

REENIE. Mom, that's what all the boys do at intermission time. They take girls and go out to the cars. Some of them don't even come back for the rest of the dance.

CORA. But are you sure Sammy did that? Did you see him?

REENIE. No, Mom, I just know that's what he did.

CORA. Wouldn't *you* have gone out to one of the cars with him?

REENIE. (*With self-disparagement*) Oh, Mom.

CORA. What makes you say "Oh, Mom" that way?

REENIE. He wouldn't have liked *me* that way.

CORA. But why? Why not?

REENIE. I'm just not *hot stuff* like the other girls.

CORA. Reenie, what an expression! You're pretty. You're every bit as pretty as Flirt or Mary Jane. Half a woman's beauty is in her confidence.

REENIE. Oh, Mom.

CORA. Reenie, I've tried to raise you proper, but . . . you're sixteen now. It's perfectly natural if a boy wants to kiss you, and you let him. It's all right if you *like* the boy.

REENIE. (*A hesitant admission*) Oh . . . Sammy kissed me.

CORA. (*Quite surprised*) He did?

REENIE. On the way out to the party in Punky's car. Flirt and Punky were in the front seat, Sammy and I in the back. Punky had a flask . . .

CORA. The little devil!

REENIE. Mom, most of those wealthy boys who go away to college are kind of wild.

CORA. Go on.

REENIE. Well, Punky and Flirt started necking, very first thing. Flirt, I don't mean to be tattling, but she *is* kind of fast.

CORA. I guessed as much. You aren't tattling.

REENIE. Well, Sammy and I felt kind of embarrassed, with no one else to talk to, and so he took my hand. Oh, he was very nice about it, Mom. And then he put an arm around me, and said . . . "May I kiss you, Reenie?" And I was so surprised, I said "yes" before I knew *what* I was saying. And he kissed me. Was it all right, Mom?

CORA. Did you like the young man? That's the important thing.

REENIE. Yes, I . . . I liked him . . . very much. (*She sobs helplessly*) Oh, Mom.

CORA. (*Going to Reenie*) There, there Reenie dear. If he's the kind of young man who goes around kissing all the girls, you don't want to worry about him any more. You did right to leave the party!

REENIE. Did I, Mom?

CORA. Of course you did. I'm very disappointed in Sammy. I thought he was such a nice boy. But I guess appearances can be deceiving.

REENIE. Oh Mom!

CORA. There, there dear. There are plenty of other young men in the world. You're young. You're not going to have to worry.

REENIE. (*Struggling to her feet*) Mom, I don't think I ever want to get married.

CORA. Reenie!

REENIE. I mean it, Mom.

CORA. You're too young to make a decision like that.

REENIE. I'm serious.

CORA. What makes you say such a thing? Tell me.

REENIE. I don't want to fight with anyone, like you and Daddy.

CORA. Oh, God.

REENIE. Every time you and Daddy fight, I just feel that the whole house is going to cave in all around me.

CORA. Then I *am* to blame.

REENIE. And I think I'd be lots happier, just by myself, teaching school, or working in an office building.

CORA. No, daughter. You need someone after you grow up. You need someone.

REENIE. But I don't want to. I don't *want* to need anyone, ever in my life. It's a horrible feeling to need someone.

CORA. (*Disturbed*) Daughter!

REENIE. Anyway, the only times I'm really happy are when I'm alone, practicing at the piano or studying in the library.

CORA. Weren't you happy last night when Sammy kissed you?

REENIE. I guess you can't count on happiness like that.

CORA. Daughter, when you start getting older, you'll find yourself getting lonely and you'll want someone; someone who'll hear you if you get sick and cry out in the night; and someone to give you love and let you give your love back to him in return. Oh, I'd hate to see any child of mine miss that in life. (*There is a moment of quiet realization between them. Then we hear the sound of a motor car drawing up to the house. Cora is excited as a girl, running to the window*) That must be your father! No, it's Sonny. In a big limousine. He's getting out of the car as if he owned it. Mrs. Stanford must have sent him home with her chauffeur. (*She gives chauffeur its American pronunciation*) (*Sonny, in his Sunday suit, bursts into the house R. waving a five-dollar bill in his mother's face*)

SONNY. Mom. Look Mom! Mrs. Stanford gave me five dollars for speaking my piece. See? Five whole dollars. She said I was the most talented little boy she ever saw. See, Mom? Then she got out her pocketbook and gave me five whole dollars. See?

CORA. I declare. Why, Sonny, I'm proud of you, Boy. That's the very first money you ever earned and I'm very proud.

SONNY. And Mrs. Stanford sent me home with her chauffeur, too, Mom. (*He gives the word its French pronunciation*) That's the way you're supposed to pronounce it, chauffeur. It's French.

CORA. If you spend any more time at Mrs. Stanford's, you'll be getting too high hat to come home. (*She notices Reenie starting upstairs*) We'll talk later, Reenie. (*Reenie off L. Cora turns her attention again to Sonny*) Did you have anything to eat?

SONNY. Oh, Mom, it was just delicious. She had all kinds of little sandwiches. Gee, they were good. And cocoa, too, Mom, with lots of whipped cream on top, in little white cups with gold edges. Gee, they were pretty. And lots of little cakes too, with pink frosting and green. And ice cream too. I just ate and ate and ate.

CORA. Good. That means I won't have to get you any supper.

SONNY. No. I don't want any supper. I'm going to the movies tonight. And to the Royal Candy Kitchen afterwards, to buy myself a great big sundae with chocolate and marshmallow and cherries and . . .

CORA. Now wait a minute, Sonny. This is the first money you've ever earned in your life, and I think you should save it.

SONNY. Oh, Mom!

CORA. I mean it. Five dollars is a lot of money, and I'm not going to let you squander it on movies and sundaes. You'll thank me for this some day. (*She takes his piggy bank from the bookcase R.*)

SONNY. I will not. I will not thank you!

CORA. Sonny. (*She takes the bill from him and drops it into the bank. Sonny is wild with injustice*)

SONNY. Look what you've done. I hate you! I wanta see the movie. I've just gotta see the movie. If I can't see the movie I'll kill myself.

CORA. Such foolish talk!

SONNY. I mean it. I'll kill myself.

CORA. Now be quiet, Sonny. I want to have a little talk.

SONNY. Can I sell the milk bottles for money?

CORA. (*Sitting at table C.*) No! Now quit pestering me about the movies. You've already talked me into letting you see one movie this week. I have scarcely any money now, and I can't spare a cent. (*Sonny is badly frustrated. He finds the favors that Sammy promised him, displayed on the settee. He throws a handfull of confetti recklessly in the air, then dons a paper hat, and blows violently on a paper horn*) Sonny! Stop that racket! You're going to have to clean up that mess.

SONNY. You won't let me have any fun at all.

CORA. The young man was very thoughtful to have sent you the favors. I wish he had been as thoughtful in other ways.

SONNY. Didn't Reenie have a good time at the party last night?

CORA. No.

SONNY. Serves her right. Serves her right.

CORA. Sonny! I'm not going to have any more talk like that. If you and your sister can't get along, you can at least have a little respect for one another. Now, come here, Sonny, I want to talk serious for a little while. (*Sonny taunts her with the horn*) Will you go sit down?

SONNY. What's the matter? (*He sits opposite her at table C.*)

CORA. Nothing, I just want to talk a while.

SONNY. (*Suddenly solemn and apprehensive*) Have I done something bad?

CORA. Well, I don't know if you have or if I have. Anyway, we've got to talk about it. Sonny, you mustn't come crawling into my bed any more. I let you do it last night, but I shouldn't have. It was wrong.

SONNY. I was scared.

CORA. Just the same, that's not to happen again, Sonny. It's not the same when a boy your age comes crawling into bed with his mother. You can't expect me to mean as much to you as when you were a baby. Can you understand, Sonny? (*He looks away from her with unconscious guilt. She studies him*) I think you're older in your feelings than I ever realized. You're a funny mixture, Sonny. In some ways shy as your sister. In other ways, bold as a pirate.

SONNY. I don't like you any more at all.

CORA. Sonny!

SONNY. I don't care. You make me mad.

CORA. (*Going to him*) Oh God, I've kept you too close to me, Sonny. Too close. I'll take the blame, boy. But don't be mad. Your mother still loves you, Sonny. (*But she sees that they are at an impasse*) Well, we won't talk about it any more. Run along to the store now before it closes. (*We see Flirt's face in the door window R. She is knocking on the door and calling for Reenie. Cora hurries to open the door*)

CORA. Flirt!

FLIRT. (*Rushing inside*) Where's Reenie? . . . Reenie. Oh, Mrs. Flood, I have the most awful news.

CORA. What is it, Flirt?

FLIRT. (*Flirt's face, her whole body, are contorted by shock and confused grief*) Oh, it's so awful.

CORA. Tell me.

FLIRT. Is Reenie here? I've got to tell her, too.

CORA. (*Calls upstairs*) Reenie, can you come down? Flirt is here.

REENIE. I'm coming. (*Off L.*)

FLIRT. Oh Mrs. Flood, it's the most awful thing that ever happened in this town. It's the most awful thing I ever heard of happening anywhere.

CORA. Did something happen to you, or your family . . . ?

FLIRT: No, it's Sammy.

CORA. Sammy . . . ?

REENIE. (*Coming down stairs L.*) What is it, Flirt?

FLIRT. Kid! Sammy Goldenbaum . . . killed himself. (*There is a long silence*) (*Reenie goes to the chair D.L.*)

CORA. Where did you hear this, Flirt?

FLIRT. Mrs. Givens told me. The hotel people over in Oklahoma City called her about it just a little while ago. They found a letter in Sammy's suitcase Mrs. Givens had written him, inviting him to come home with Punky.

CORA. Oklahoma City?

FLIRT. He went over there last night after he left the party. He took the midnight train. That's what they figured out, because he registered at the hotel this morning at two o'clock.

CORA. How . . . did he do it, Flirt?

FLIRT. (*She hides her face in her hands as though hiding from the hideous reality of it*) He . . . Oh, I just can't.

CORA. There, there, Honey.

FLIRT. Oh, I'm such a silly about things. He . . . he jumped out of the window . . . on the fourteenth floor . . . and landed on the pavement below.

CORA. Oh, my God.

FLIRT. Oh . . . it's really the most terrible thing that ever happened to me. I never did know anyone who killed himself before.

66

CORA. Does anyone have any idea what made him do it?

FLIRT. No! Punky says that he used to get kind of moody at times, but Punky never expected him to do anything like *this*.

CORA. Why did he go to Oklahoma City in the middle of the night?

FLIRT. No one knows that either . . . for sure. But one thing did happen at the party. He was dancing with Mary Jane Ralston . . . that cow . . . just before intermission . . . and Mrs. Ralston . . . she'd had too much to drink . . . comes out in the middle of the floor and stops them.

CORA. What for?

FLIRT. Well, you know how Mrs. Ralston is. No one takes her very serious even if she does have money. Anyway she came right out in the middle of the floor and gave Sammy a bawling out.

CORA. A bawling out? Why?

FLIRT. She said she wasn't giving this party for Jews, and she didn't intend for her daughter to dance with a Jew, and besides, Jews weren't allowed in the Country Club anyway. And that's not so. They are too allowed in the Country Club. Maybe they're not permitted to be members, but they're certainly allowed as guests. Everyone knows that. (*She turns now to Reenie, who has sat numb in a chair since Flirt's shocking announcement*) Where were you when it all happened?

REENIE. I . . . I . . . (*But she is inarticulate*)

CORA. Reenie wasn't feeling well. She left the party and came home.

FLIRT. The other kids told me Sammy was looking for you everywhere. He was going around asking everyone, where's Reenie?

CORA. That . . . that's too bad.

FLIRT. (*Turning to Cora*) . . . but a thing like that isn't serious enough to make a boy kill himself, is it?

CORA. Well . . . he did.

FLIRT. An old blabber mouth like Mrs. Ralston?

CORA. She was a stranger to Sammy. She probably sounded like the voice of the world.

FLIRT. Gee . . . I just don't understand things like that. Do you know something else, Mrs. Flood? They called Sammy's mother way out in California, and told her, and I guess she was terribly sorry and everything, but she told them to go on and have the funeral in Oklahoma City, that she'd pay all the expenses, but she wouldn't be able to come for it because she was working. And she cried over the telephone and asked them please to try to keep her name out of the papers, because she said it wasn't generally known that she had a son.

CORA. There won't be anyone Sammy knows at the funeral, will there?

FLIRT. Mrs. Givens said Punky and his daddy could drive us over for it. Will you come, Reenie? Do you wanta come, too, Sonny? Well . . . it'll be day after tomorrow, in the afternoon. We'll all have to get excused from school. Oh gee, it all makes me feel so kind of *strange*. Doesn't it *you*, kid? I think I'll go to Sunday School tomorrow. Do you wanta go with me, Reenie? (*Reenie nods yes*) Oh, I feel just terrible. (*Flirt bolts out the front door R., as though wanting to run away from all that is tragic or sorrowful in life. Cora keeps silent for several moments, her eyes on Reenie*)

CORA. Where were you when Sammy went off?

REENIE. (*Twisting with grief*) Stop it Mom!

CORA. Tell me. Where were you?

REENIE. Don't Mom!

CORA. (*Very insistent*) *Tell* me.

REENIE. I . . . was up in . . . the girls' room.

CORA. Where did you leave Sammy?

REENIE. As soon as we got to the party, Sammy and I started dancing. He danced three straight dances with me, Mom. Nobody cut in. I didn't think anybody was ever going to cut in, Mom. I got to feeling so humiliated I didn't know what to do. I just couldn't bear for Sammy to think that no one liked me.

CORA. Dear God!

REENIE. So I told Sammy there was someone at the party I had to talk to. Then I took him over to Mary Jane Ralston and . . . introduced him to her . . . and told him to dance with her.

CORA. Reenie!

REENIE. I . . . I thought he'd like her.

CORA. But you said that *you* liked Sammy. You told me you did.

REENIE. But Mom, I just couldn't *bear* for him to think I was such a wallflower.

68

CORA. You ran off and *hid,* when an ounce of thoughtfulness, one or two kind words might have saved him.
REENIE. I didn't *know.* I didn't *know.*
CORA. A nice young man like that, bright and pleasant, handsome as a prince, caught out here in this sandy soil without a friend to his name and no one to turn to when some thoughtless fool attacks him and he takes it to heart. (*Reenie sobs uncontrollably*) Tears aren't going to do any good now, Reenie. Now you listen to me. I've heard all I intend to listen to about being so shy and sensitive and afraid of people. I can't respect those feelings any more. They're nothing but selfishness. (*Reenie starts to bolt from the room just as Flirt did, but Cora's voice holds her*) Reenie! It's a fine thing when we have so little confidence in ourselves, we can't stop to think of the other person.
SONNY. (*Who has been a silent listener until now*) I *hate* people.
CORA. Sonny!
SONNY. I *do.*
CORA. Then you're just as bad as Peg Ralston.
SONNY. How can you keep from hating?
CORA. There are all kinds of people in the world. And you have to live with them all. God never promised us any different. The bad people, you don't hate. You're only sorry they have to be. Now, run along to the store before it closes. (*Sonny goes out R., and finds himself again confronted by the jeers of the neighborhood boys, that sound like the voices that have plagued humanity from the beginning of time*)
BOYS' VOICES (*Off R.*)
Sissy Sonny!
Sonny Flood! His name is mud!
Sonny plays with dolls!
Sonny loves his mama!
(*Hearing the voices, Cora runs to the door R., but stops herself from going further*)
CORA. I guess I can't go through life protecting him from bullies. (*She goes to Reenie*) I'm sorry I spoke so harshly to you, Reenie.
REENIE. He asked for *me* . . . for *me.* The only time anyone ever *wanted* me, or *needed* me in my entire life. And I wasn't there. I

didn't stop once to think of . . . Sammy. I've always thought I was the only person in the world who had any feelings at all.

CORA. Well . . . you're not, if that's any comfort. Where are you going, dear?

REENIE. (*Resignedly*) I haven't done anything to my room all day. I . . . I still have to make my bed. (*Reenie exits upstairs L.*)

CORA. It's Saturday. Change the linens. I put them in the attic to dry. (*Cora goes into the parlor U.C. to pull down the shades. Rubin enters from the dining room U.L. in his stocking feet, carrying several bags which he drops onto the floor with a clatter. Cora comes running from the parlor*) My God!

RUBIN. I scare ya?

CORA. Rubin! I hate to be frightened so.

RUBIN. I didn't *mean* to frighten ya.

CORA. I didn't hear you drive in.

RUBIN. I didn't.

CORA. Where's the car?

RUBIN. It ain't runnin' right. Left it down town at the garage. I walked home.

CORA. Why did you come in the back way?

RUBIN. Cora, what difference does it make if I came in the back way or the front way, or down the chimney? My boots was covered with mud, so I left 'em out on the back porch. I din wanta track up your nice, clean house. Now, wasn't that thoughtful of me?

CORA. Did you get my message?

RUBIN. What message?

CORA. Oh . . . nothing.

RUBIN. What message you talkin' about?

CORA. The route you left me said you'd be in Blackwell last night. I called you there, but . . . Well, I suppose you had better places to be.

RUBIN. That's right. I did. What'd ya call me for?

CORA. (*Hurt*) I don't know now. You'll be wanting a hot bath. I'll go turn on the water tank. (*Cora exits through dining room door U.L. Rubin sits in his big chair D.L. and drops his face into his hands with a look of sad discouragement. Then he begins to unpack one of the bags, taking out small pieces of harness and toss-*

70

ing them on the floor. In a few moments, Cora returns U.L.) What
made you decide to come back?
RUBIN. I lost my job.
CORA. What?
RUBIN. I said I lost my job.
CORA. Rubin! You've always sold more harness for the company
than any of the other salesmen.
RUBIN. Yah, the oney trouble is, *no* one's selling much harness
today because no one's buyin' it. People are buyin' automobiles.
Harness salesmen are . . . things of the past.
CORA. Do you mean . . . your company's going out of business?
RUBIN. That's it! You won the kewpie doll.
CORA. Oh, Rubin!
RUBIN. So that's why ya couldn't get me in Blackwell last night.
I went somewhere else, regardless of what you were thinkin',
lookin' for a job.
CORA. *(A little embarrassed with regret)* Oh . . . I apologize,
Rubin.
RUBIN. Oh, that's all right. You have to get in your li'l digs ev'ry
once in a while. I'm used to 'em.
CORA. I'm really awfully sorry. Believe me.
RUBIN. I was in Tulsa, talkin' to some men at the Southwest
Supply Company. They're hirin' lotsa new men to go out in the
fields and sell their equipment.
CORA. *(Seizing her opportunity)* Rubin Flood, now that you've
lost one travelling job, I'm not going to let you take another. You
go down town the first thing Monday morning and talk to John
Fraser. He's bought out all the Curley Cue markets in town, and
he needs men to manage them. He'd give you a job in a minute.
Now you do what I say, Rubin.
RUBIN. *(He looks at her for several moments before speaking)*
God damn! I come home here t'apologize to you for hittin' ya.
I been feelin' all week like the meanest critter alive, because I took
a sock at a woman. My wife, at that. I walked in here ready to *beg*
ya to forgive me. Now, I feel like doin' it all over again. Don't
you realize you can't talk to a man like that? Don't you realize
that every time you talk that way, I just gotta *go* out and raise
more hell, just to prove to myself I'm a free man? Don't you know

71

that when you talk to a man like that, you're not givin' him credit for havin' any brains, or any guts, or a spine, or . . . or a few other body parts that are pretty important, too? All these years we been married, you never once really admitted to yourself what kinda man I am. No, ya keep talkin' to me like I was the kinda man you think I *oughta* be. (*He grabs her by the shoulders*) Look at me. Don't you know who I am? Don't you know who I am?

CORA. Rubin, you're hurting me.

RUBIN. I'm takin' the job if I can get it. It's a damn good job, pays good money.

CORA. I don't care about money.

RUBIN. No, you don't! Not until you see Peg Ralston come waltzin' down the street in a new fur coat, and then you start wonderin' why old Rubin don't shoot hisself in the foot to make a lot of money.

CORA. Rubin, I promise you I'll never envy Peg Ralston another thing, as long as I live.

RUBIN. Did it ever occur to you that maybe I feel like a cheapskate because I can't buy you no fur coat? Did you ever stop to think maybe I'd like to be able to send my kids away to a fine college?

CORA. All I'm asking is for you to give them something of *yourself.*

RUBIN. God damn it! What have *I* got to give 'em? In this day and age, what's a man like me got to give? With the whole world so all fired crazy about makin' money, how can *any* man, unless he's got a million dollars stuck in his pocket, feel he's got anything else to give that's very important?

CORA. Rubin!

RUBIN. I mean it, Cora.

CORA. I never realized you had such doubts.

RUBIN. The new job is work I've never done. Work I never even thought of doin'. Learnin' about all that God damn machinery, and how to get out there and demonstrate it. Working with different kinds of men, that's smarter than I am, that think fast and talk sharp and mean all business. Men I can't sit around and chew tobacco with and joke with like I did m'old customers. I . . . I don't like 'em. I don't know if I'm *gonna* like them.

CORA. But you just said you wanted the job.

RUBIN. I don't like them, but I'm gonna join them. A fellow's gotta get into the swim. There's nothing else to do. But I'm scared. I don't know how I'll make out. I . . . I'm scared.

CORA. I never supposed you had it *in* you to fear.

RUBIN. I s'pose all this time you been thinkin' you was married to one a them movin' pitcher fellas that jump off bridges and hold up trains and shoot Indians, and are never scared a nothin'. Times are changin', Cora, and I dunno where they're goin'. When I was a boy, there wasn't much more to this town than a post office. I on'y had six years a schoolin' cause that's all the Old Man thought I'd ever need. Now look at things. School buildin's, churches, fine stores, movie theatres, a country club. Men becomin' millionaires overnight, drivin' down the street in big limousines, goin' out to the country club and gettin' drunk, acting like they was the lords of creation. I dunno what to think now, Cora. I'm a stranger in the very land I was born in.

CORA. (*Trying to restore his pride*) Your folks pioneered this country.

RUBIN. Sometimes I wonder if it's not a lot easier to pioneer a country that it is to settle down in it. I look at the town now and don't recognize anything in it. I come home here, and I still have to get used to the piano, and the telephone, and the gas stove, and the lace curtains at the windows, the carpets on the floor. All these things are still *new* to me. I dunno what to make of 'em. How can *I* feel I've got anything to give to my children when the world's as strange to me as it is to them?

CORA. (*With a new awareness of him*) Rubin!

RUBIN. I'm doin' the best I can, Cora. Can't ya understand that? I'm doin' the best I can.

CORA. Yes Rubin . . . I know you are.

RUBIN. Now, there's a few more things I gotta say. . . . I wanna apologize. I'm sorry I hit ya, Cora. I'm awfully sorry.

CORA. I know I provoked you, Rubin.

RUBIN. You provoked me, but . . . I still shouldn'ta hit ya. It wasn't manly.

CORA. I'm not holding it against you, Rubin.

RUBIN. And I'm sorry I made such a fuss about gettin' the girl a new dress. But I was awful worried about losin' my job then, and I din have much money left in the bank.

CORA. Rubin, if I'd known that, I wouldn't have *thought* of buying the dress. You should have told me, Rubin.

RUBIN. I din wanta make you worry, too.

CORA. But that's what I'm for.

RUBIN. That's all I gotta say, except that . . . I love ya. You're a good woman and I couldn't git along without you.

CORA. I love you, too, Rubin. And I couldn't get along without you another day.

RUBIN. You're clean, and dainty. Give a man a feeling of decency . . . and order . . . and respect.

CORA. Thank you, Rubin.

RUBIN. Just don't get the idea you can rearrange *me* like ya do the house, whenever ya wanta put it in order.

CORA. I'll remember. (*There is a short silence between them now that follows their new understanding*) When you have fears about things, please tell me, Rubin.

RUBIN. It's hard for a man t' admit his fears, even to hisself.

CORA. Why? Why?

RUBIN. He's always afraid of endin' up like . . . like your brother-in-law Morris.

CORA. Oh! (*Cora has a new appreciation of him. She runs to him, throwing her arms about him in a fast embrace. A glow of satisfaction radiates from Rubin, to have his woman back in his arms*)

RUBIN. Oh my goodness. (*Rubin carries Cora C., where they sit like honeymooners, she on his lap, and he kisses her. Sonny returns R. now with a sack of groceries, and stands staring at his parents until they become aware of him*) H'lo, son.

SONNY. Hi!

CORA. Take the groceries to the kitchen, Sonny. (*Sonny obeys*) Rubin, Mrs. Stanford paid Sonny five dollars this afternoon for speaking a piece at her tea party.

RUBIN. I'll be damned. He'll be makin' more money than his Old Man. (*Sonny exits now through dining room door U.L.*)

CORA. Be nice to him, Rubin. Show him you want to be his friend.

RUBIN. I'm nice to that boy, ain't I?

CORA. Sometimes you do talk awfully rough and bad natured.

RUBIN. Well . . . *life's* rough. *Life's* bad natured.

CORA. I know. And I keep trying to pretend it isn't.

RUBIN. I'll remind ya.

CORA. Every time I see the kids go out of the house, I worry, like I was watching them go out into life, and they seem so young and helpless.

RUBIN. But ya gotta let 'em go, Cora. Ya gotta let 'em go.

CORA. I've always felt I could give them life like a present, all wrapped in white, with every promise of happiness inside.

RUBIN. That ain't the way it works.

CORA. No. All I can promise them is life itself. (*With this realization, she gets off Rubin's lap*) I'd better go to the kitchen and put the groceries away.

RUBIN. (*Grabs her to him, not willing to let her go*) T'hell with the groceries!

CORA. (*A maidenly protest*) Rubin!

RUBIN. (*Caressing her*) Is there any chance of us bein' alone t'night?

CORA. (*Secretively*) I think Reenie plans to go to the library. If you give Sonny a dime, I'm sure he'll go to the movie.

RUBIN. It's a deal. (*He tries again to re-engage her in lovemaking*)

CORA. Now Rubin, be patient. (*She exits through dining room door U.L. as Reenie comes running downstairs L.*)

REENIE. Did I hear Daddy?

RUBIN. Hello, daughter.

REENIE. (*She runs into his arms and he lifts her high in the air*) Oh, Daddy!

RUBIN. Well, how's my girl?

REENIE. I feel better now that you're home, Daddy.

RUBIN. Thank ya, daughter.

REENIE. I've been practicing a new piece, Daddy. It's Chopin. Do you want me to play it for you?

RUBIN. Sure. I like sweet music same as everyone.

REENIE. I can't play it quite perfect yet, but almost. (*Reenie goes into parlor U.C. and in a moment we hear another wistful piece of Chopin*)

RUBIN. That's all right. (*Sonny now returns U.L. and stands far*

R. Rubin C. faces him. They look at each other with wonder and just a little resentment. But Rubin goes to Sonny, making the effort to offer himself) Son, your mom tells me you do real well, goin' around speaking pieces, gettin' to be a reg'lar Jackie Coogan. I got a customer has a daughter does real well at thet kind a thing Gets up before people and whistles.

SONNY. Whistles?

RUBIN. Yah! Like birds. Every kinda bird ya ever heard of. Maybe you'd like to meet her sometime.

SONNY. Oh, maybe. *(Rubin feels himself on uncertain ground)*

RUBIN. Your mom said maybe you'd like to go to the movie tonight. I guess I could spare you the money. *(He digs into his pocket)*

SONNY. I've changed my mind. I don't want to now. *(Sonny turns from his father now)*

RUBIN. *(Rubin looks at his son as though realizing the break. With a feeling of failure, he puts a warm hand on Sonny's shoulder)* Oh! Well, I ain't gonna argue. *(Now he passes the parlor and speaks to Reenie)* That's real purty, Daughter.

REENIE. Thank you, Daddy.

RUBIN. *(Opens dining room door U.L. and speaks to Cora)* Cora, those kids ain't goin' to the movies. Come on now.

CORA. I'll be up in a minute, Rubin.

RUBIN. *(Closing the door behind him, speaking to Reenie and Sonny)* I'm goin' upstairs now, and have my bath. *(Reenie and Sonny watch him all the way upstairs)*

SONNY. They always want to be alone.

REENIE. All married people do, Crazy. *(Sonny impulsively sticks out his tongue at her. But she ignores him, picking up one of the favors, a reminder of Sammy, and fondling it tenderly. Sonny begins to feel regret)*

SONNY. I'm sorry I made a face at you, Reenie.

REENIE. *(Sobbing softly)* Go on and make as many faces as you like. I'm not going to fight with you anymore.

SONNY. Don't cry, Reenie.

REENIE. I didn't know Sammy had even remembered the favors until I started to go. Then I went to find my jacket, and there they were, sticking out of my pocket. At the very moment he **was** putting them there . . . he must have had in mind doing what he did.

SONNY. (*With a burst of new generosity*) *You! You* keep the favors, Reenie.

REENIE. He promised them to *you*.

SONNY. Just the same . . . *you* keep them, Reenie.

REENIE. Do you mean it?

SONNY. Yes.

REENIE. You never were thoughtful like this . . . before. (*Cora comes through the dining room door U.L. now, hears the children's plans and stands unobserved, listening*)

SONNY. Reenie, do you want to go to the movie tonight? It's Mae Murray in "Fascination," and there's an Our Gang Comedy first.

REENIE. I don't feel I should.

SONNY. When I feel bad, I just *have* to go to the movies. I just *have* to.

REENIE. I was supposed to go to the library tonight.

SONNY. Please go with me, Reenie. Please.

REENIE. Do you really want me?

SONNY. Yes, Reenie. Yes.

REENIE. Where would you get the money to take *me*, Sonny? I have to pay adult admission. It's thirty-five cents.

SONNY. I've got all the money we'll need. (*He runs for his piggy bank R., Cora making a quick return to dining room U.L.*)

REENIE. Sonny! Mother told you you had to save that money.

SONNY. I don't care. She's not going to boss me for the rest of my life. It's *my* money, and I've got a right to spend it. (*With a heroic gesture of defiance, he throws the piggy bank smashing onto the fireplace, its pieces scattering on the floor*)

REENIE. Sonny!

SONNY. (*Finding his five-dollar bill in the rubble*) And we'll have enough for pop corn, too, and for ice cream afterwards at the Royal Candy Kitchen. (*Now we see Cora in the parlor U.C., a silent witness*)

REENIE. I feel very proud to be treated by my little brother.

SONNY. Let's hurry. The comedy starts at 7:00 o'clock and I don't want to miss it.

REENIE. We can stay for the second show if we miss the comedy.

SONNY. Oh, I want to stay for the second show, anyway. I always see the comedy twice.

CORA. (*Coming forth now U.C.*) Are you children going some place?

REENIE. We're going to the movie, Mom.

CORA. Together?

REENIE. Yes.

CORA. Well . . . that's nice.

REENIE. Darn it. I left my rubbers out on the porch. (*Exits R.*)

RUBIN. (*From upstairs*) Cora!

CORA. I'll be up in a minute, Rubin. (*She turns thoughtfully to her son*) Have you forgiven your mother, Sonny?

SONNY. (*Inscrutable*) Oh . . . maybe.

CORA. Your mother still loves you, Sonny. (*She puts an arm around him but he avoids her embrace*)

SONNY. Don't, Mom.

CORA. All right. I understand.

RUBIN. (*Upstairs, growing more impatient*) Cora! Come on, Honey!

CORA. (*Calling back to him*) I'll be up in a minute, Rubin. (*Sonny looks at her with accusing eyes*) Goodbye, Sonny! (*Reenie sticks her head in from outside*)

REENIE. Hurry up, Sonny!

RUBIN. Come on, Cora! (*Cora starts up the stairs to her husband, stopping for one final look at her departing son. And Sonny, just before going out the door R., stops for one final look at his mother, his face full of confused understanding. Then he hurries out to Reenie, and Cora, like a shy maiden, starts up the stairs where we see Rubin's naked feet standing in the warm light*)

CORA. I'm coming, Rubin. I'm coming.

CURTAIN

PROPERTY PLOT

ACT I

Center:
Wicker table
Table lamp
Wicker chairs (2)
Player piano (in parlor U.C.)
Sewing basket (Cora)
  Sock
  Needle and thread
Stage Right:
Footstool
Scrapbook (Sonny)
  (in bookshelves)
Bookshelves
Stage Left: (downstage)
Leather armchair

Table (desk)
Pint of whiskey (in table drawer)
Telephone
Off Left:
Wallet (Rubin) with paper money
Suitcase (Rubin)
Off Right:
Large dress box (Flirt)
Party dress (Reenie) with price
  tag attached
Wristwatch (Flirt)
Sack of Groceries (Sonny)
Mirror on wall
Picture of Cora's family on wall

ACT II

Off Left:
Dish (Reenie)
Dish Towel (Reenie)
Vase (Sonny)
Paperbag filled with Fried Chicken
  (Cora)
  Gizzard
  Drumstick
Cup of flour paste (Sonny)
Plate of cookies (Lottie)
Wray (Sunday coat) (Reenie)
Off Right:
Small package containing perfume

  bottle (Morris)
Flask (Punky)
Swords and scabbards (2 each)
Stage Center:
Scrapbook (Sonny) (in parlor)
Platform (Sonny) (in parlor)
Personal:
Pack of life savers (Morris)
Corset (Lottie)
Hand Puzzle (Morris)
Strike—from Act I
Large dress box (Reenie)
Party dress (Reenie)

ACT III

Stage Left:
Tray with lunch dishes (on table
  D.L.)
Towel (Reenie)
Stage Right:
Piggie Bank (in bookshelf)
Party Favors (on footstool—settee)
  Confetti
  Paper Hat
  Paper Horn

Off Left:
Suitcases (2) (Rubin)
  Harness parts in one suitcase
Off Right:
Sack of groceries (Sonny)
Five dollar bill (Sonny
There is a fire in fireplace D.L.
Strike—from Act II
  Cup of flour paste
  Plate of cookies
  Scrapbook

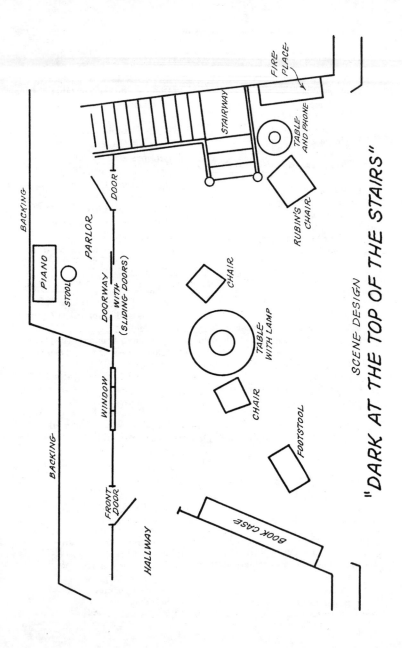

SCENE DESIGN

"DARK AT THE TOP OF THE STAIRS"